W9-APQ-846

Works and Days

and

Theogony

HESIOD

Works and Days

and

Theogony

Translated by
Stanley Lombardo
Introduction and Notes by
Robert Lamberton

Hackett Publishing Company, Inc.
Indianapolis/Cambridge

Hesiod: *fl. ca.* 800 B.C.

Copyright © 1993 by Hackett Publishing Company, Inc.

All rights reserved
Printed in the United States of America

21 20 19 18 17   7 8 9 10 11 12

Cover art by Anne Carson
Interior design by Dan Kirklin

For further information, please address
  Hackett Publishing Company, Inc.
  P.O. Box 44937
  Indianapolis, Indiana 46244-0937

  www.hackettpublishing.com

Library of Congress Cataloging-in-Publication Data
Hesiod.
      [Works and days]
      Works and days; Theogony / Hesiod; translated by Stanley Lombardo;
      with introduction, notes, and glossary by Robert Lamberton.
            p.   cm.
      ISBN 0-87220-180-5 (cloth).   ISBN 0-87220-179-1 (paper).
      1. Hesiod—Translations into English.   2. Mythology, Greek—
Poetry.   3. Gods, Greek—Poetry.   I. Lombardo, Stanley, 1943–
IV. Title.   V. Title: Theogony.
PA4010.E5   1993
881'.01—dc20
                                                            93-24545
                                                                CIP

ISBN-13: 978-0-87220-180-4 (cloth)
ISBN-13: 978-0-87220-179-8 (pbk.)

CONTENTS

This translation is dedicated to the memory of my father

Peter Lombardo

who understood justice and hard work

INTRODUCTION

The *Theogony* and *Works and Days* stand alongside the *Iliad* and *Odyssey* at the beginning of the European literary tradition. It is probable that the three poems that come down under the name of Hesiod—an account of the origins of the divine order, a collection of agricultural wisdom poetry, and a mini-epic called *The Shield of Herakles*[1]—along with the epics of the Trojan War and of Odysseus' return home, assigned by tradition to the blind bard Homer, were all assembled at roughly the same time in something like the form in which we have them today. That time is unlikely to have been earlier than 800 BCE or much later than 600.

In the *Frogs* (405 BCE), Aristophanes has the tragic poet Aeschylus recite the pedigree of poet educators:

> Look how right from the start
> the noble poets have been useful—been teachers:
> Orpheus taught us initiations and avoidance of bloodletting,
> Mousaios taught divination and cures for sickness, and Hesiod,
> the working of the soil and the seasons of harvest and plowing.
> And divine Homer—where else did he get his honor and glory,
> except from teaching tactics, military virtues, and the arming of
> heroes?
>
> (1030–34)

The context is comic and the descriptions reductive, but this stereotypic account of archaic Greek poetry from a classical perspective tells us a great deal about Greek cultural traditions. The list is not idiosyncratic—they are the same four poets Plato has Socrates imagine talking with in the other world (*Apology* 41a). To the age of Pericles, Hesiod was one of four mythic bards standing at the source of Greek tradition. His special province was farming, and there were those who believed that of the many poems attributed to him, the only one that was truly his was the *Works and Days*. It is only in the *Theogony* that the speaker identifies himself as *Hesiodos*, but only in the *Works and Days* does he emerge as an individualized human being with a story and a characteristic, idiosyncratic view of the world.

---

1. Of these three poems, the first two are included here. The third is less often read, and the arguments for Hesiodic authorship are less compelling.

1

The Rustic Bard

The singer of the *Works and Days* has a remarkable amount to say about himself, and it is information of a sort unprecedented in Greek poetry. He claims first of all that his father (whom he does not name) came from the coast of Asia Minor, and specifically from the city called Kyme. This was a settlement of Aeolic speakers, whose dialect was that of the Greeks of the northwest corner of Asia Minor, including the island of Lesbos. Kyme was located, however, considerably to the south of the other Aeolic cities, not far north of Smyrna (one of the cities that claimed Homer as a native son) and most of the Greeks of the area were Ionic speakers. Kyme is very much a part of the real world and not a fiction. You can visit the ruins by driving a little more than an hour north of Izmir, along the coast. The attractive bay where the remains are located has recently been developed as a port with an oil refinery, but the site still has a certain charm. The coastline has sunk since antiquity, and the waves come right up into town, exposing foundations and a great deal of pottery, including an unusual percentage of a distinctive Hellenistic shape called the "fish plate." It seems that half a millennium after Hesiod's father's time, his hometown had a remarkable strip of fish restaurants.

What was it like in, say, 750 BCE? The excavations tell us little. Hesiod says his father was running from "awful poverty," but without telling us whether the community itself had come on hard times, or only his father. The father went sailing, presumably as a merchant or shipper—something Hesiod does not advise others to do, but is quite content to pontificate about. He nevertheless ended up decidedly landlocked in a dusty, remote fold of Mt. Helikon in western Boeotia, in a village called Askra (a name that, if we can believe an Alexandrian lexicographer of the fifth century CE, meant "Barrenoak"). Hesiod's description of the village is famous (*W&D* 707–10 [640]):

> bad in winter,
> > godawful in summer,
> > > nice never.

There, presumably, his sons Hesiod and Perses were born, and Hesiod as a boy, before his vocation as a poet came to him, tended sheep on the slopes of the mountain. What his brother Perses was doing meanwhile, we don't know, but since Hesiod repeatedly characterizes his brother as a lazy jerk (*nepios*) we may assume he didn't do much. Hesiod himself, though, after the turning point in his life—he describes this event as an apparition of the Muses on the slopes of Helikon—perfected his poetic performances to the point that he was a successful competitor in the funeral games of one Amphidamas, a Euboean warrior of uncertain date. At the dramatic date of the *Works and Days* (ca. 700 BCE?), their father is dead and Hesiod and Perses have gone to law over the inheritance (*W&D* 50–57 [34–41]). Perses has gotten more than his share by paying off the "bribe-eating kings", but Hesiod is not resigned to the finality of the distribution (*W&D* 50–51 [35–36]). It is hard to imagine, though, what we are to imagine that Hesiod hopes to recover from his brother, given the fact that Perses, the low-life cheat, has now come begging to *him*. (*W&D* 439 [396]).

These are the autobiographical givens, and from the summary above, it should be clear that (with the exception of Hesiod's name) they all come from the *Works and Days*. Do they have anything to do with the world outside of that poem? The poem itself—the speech the poet delivers to Perses—is by no means an intimate communication. It is a grand, often pompous, public statement, in which Perses is told things about himself and his family that he can hardly need to be told. (Think of Priam in Book 3 of the *Iliad*, having the Greek warriors on the plain identified for him, warriors whom he has been watching out there for nine years, according to Homer's fiction; clearly it is the audience of the *Iliad* that needs this information, not the king of Troy.) No, this communication between Hesiod and Perses is clearly meant for a third party, an audience, and everything it contains is shaped and articulated by the needs of that indirect communication:

speaker to addressee

to

audience

We would be rash, then, to assume that the contents of the poem—including the mute addressee Perseus—correspond to any historical reality. The *Works and Days* is a solo performance piece with two characters (only one of whom speaks). Not only Perses, but Hesiod himself, is first and foremost a fiction, and a unique one not to be found anywhere outside this poem and the prologue of the *Theogony*. Even the name, which may contain elements a native speaker would identify as descriptive of the function of the poet "casting the song," is unique. The Greek world was not full of individuals bearing the names Homer, Hesiod, Orpheus, or

Mousaios. The names of the poets at the source of the tradition were not names that could be given again and again, like Pericles or Megakles or Phainippos, but unique, honorific titles, bound to the poetry and the fictions those poems invented, elaborated, and transmitted.

Those are the reasons for caution. We do not expect the speakers of poems to be confessional or even truthful, and in the Hesiodic corpus, as we shall see, the play of reality and fiction, of art and truth, is central to the esthetic enterprise of the poetry.

There is, however, another factor in the calculation. The information Hesiod provides about himself, his father, and his brother in the *Works and Days* is of several different sorts. The relationship of Hesiod and Perses, and the whole story of the inheritance as it is woven into the advice poetry, can very easily be imagined as pure invention, a fiction that has no relationship to the real world and no function beyond the esthetic demands of the poetry itself. The proverbs, the agricultural lore, the edifying stories, the myths, are bound together into a dramatic unity of a sort by the situation the poem creates in this one-sided dramatic exchange. The speaker has all the power. He so dominates the exchange that Perses never once is allowed to open his mouth. Perses has come to beg from his brother, because he's in need. And one of the costs is that he has to listen to a condescending tirade in which he himself is repeatedly characterized as irresponsible, as a "jerk" and a do-nothing. If what he needs is a few obols to tide him over, it's clearly not going to do him much good to be told which astronomical events he has to keep an eye out for in order to know when to plow! But it comes with the package. If you have to come asking for a favor, then you have to accept the role, be addressed as someone asking for a favor, and keep quiet. On top of all this, there are old grudges, and Perses is reminded that he cheated his brother once, and as far as Hesiod is concerned, it's Perses who owes *him* something, not the other way around. This domestic drama provides a very wonderful and enlivening context for a great deal of traditional lore.

If everything in the poem were so easily susceptible to this sort of reading, no one would ever have been led to claim that Hesiod and Perses had any more historical reality than Achilles, Polyphemos, or Orpheus, creatures fabricated by the imagination and having their life only there. But there is something more in the *Works and Days*. Much of the information that fills out the story is of a specificity that makes its explanation as fiction, myth, or convention difficult. At one end of the scale of this information lies the (dramatically inappropriate and artificial) revelation that Hesiod's and Perses' father came from Aiolian Kyme. Why make *that* up? Why say it at all, unless the relationship between speaker and addressee is an authentic one, rooted in a real-world situation? This question is not easily answered (though attempts have been made to do so). There are no strong literary traditions about Kyme. Still, it is not impossible that the ideal audience of this poetry at some stage in its existence *did* have the kind of associations that would give some special flavor to this claim. It would not require much: some proverbial or stereotypic trait—affluence, poverty, cleverness, stupidity—that would turn the bit of information into something more, something meaningful or ironic or witty. Certainly, the identity of the Hesiodic speaker is built to a considerable extent on characteristic poses and attitudes, and most obviously on the cracker-barrel pessimism that makes him prone to put Perses, Askra, and the human condition in general in the worst light. But be that as it may, the fiction contains bits of "autobiographical" information that are hard to explain as other than that.

The claims made about Askra itself, and Helikon and Hesiod's experiences there, have a special place in this fiction, both in the most literal sense and perhaps in terms of its history. By their "literal" special place, I mean that they are clustered in an interesting way within the poem. Hesiod has a very marked tendency to group together the references to himself and his family with information about the Muses and about the valley of Mt. Helikon in which the town of Askra lay. In a sense, this is to be expected, but it is the role of the Muses in this complex of associations that may point to another factor that is far from obvious.

Hesiod's devotion to the Muses is a crucially important part of his poetic identity. The *Theogony* and *Works and Days* are very different poems, and there is very little to bind one to the other beyond the speaker's claims about his special relationship to the Helikonian Muses. Homer, as usual, provides the most relevant point of comparison: in the *Iliad* and *Odyssey*, the Muses are evoked several times, briefly, either to initiate the song or to assist in some special feat of memory. The poetry of Hesiod gives far more prominence to the Muses. The prologue to the *Theogony* is a hymn to the nine goddesses, recounting the story of their apparition to Hesiod on Mt. Helikon, and crediting them explicitly with conceiving and performing the Olympian prototype of the *Theogony* that the bard is about to perform. This 115-line hymn also supplies most of the rich collection of place names that give the Hesiodic corpus such an air of geographic specificity. Here alone does the name Hesiod appear in the corpus, along with the names of the streams of the Valley of the Muses (Permessos and Olmeios) and the spring Hippokrene, along with the altar of Zeus up on Helikon, all places that can be identified with features of a valley of Mt. Helikon a few miles west of Thespiai in Boeotia.

The *Works and Days* has a prologue as well, and again it is a hymn, but a much shorter one, in which the Muses are called upon to sing the praises of their father Zeus. Elsewhere in the *Works and Days*, they are mentioned only twice, in close proximity, in the passage where the singer claims to have sailed to Euboea and won a tripod (a three-legged cauldron) in the singing contest there. This tripod, he claims, he brought back and dedicated to the Helikonian Muses, who taught him song. The dedication implies a formal cult, and indeed in the Hellenistic and Roman periods, long after Hesiod's time, there was a very important cult of the Helikonian Muses in the valley west of Thespiai just mentioned, a cult associated with a festival where performers competed, at first for prizes, but eventually for mere wreaths symbolic of their prestigious victory. The story of the tripod Hesiod dedicated (which was shown to travelers in the Roman period) is very unlikely to belong to the remote period in which we must imagine any "historical" Hesiod living. It has long been considered a later addition serving the interests of the cult and the festival. Yet it is the principal link between the two poems at the heart of the corpus, or rather, between the hymnic prologue of the *Theogony*, with the story of Hesiod's vocation by the Muses, and the collection of wisdom poetry (the *Works and Days*) in which the character of the rustic bard is most richly developed, but where his name does not occur.

What conclusions can we draw? It seems clear that the festival, the poetry, and the speaker who articulates the Hesiodic poetry are interrelated. The exact nature of that relationship remains unclear, but so does the evolution in time of the Hesiodic poems. At the very least, the speaker of the *Works and Days* has been tampered with in the interests of the festival that appropriated both him and the poetry attributed to him. Just how great this institution's role in the shaping of this poetic identity may have been we cannot say, but the hymnic prologues may well have been more easily manipulated than the body of the poem. If the two hymns and the passage on the contest in Euboea are the principal—indeed, virtually the only—passages that give us a highly personalized Hesiod with a special devotion to the Helikonian Muses, then we must suspect that the role of the institution in the creation of that identity may have been considerable.

Who, then, *was* Hesiod? Somebody must have written this poetry, so why deny the claims of the text itself? The principal reason is that archaic Greek hexameter poetry constitutes a very special case in the history of the generation of poetic texts in the European tradition. There can be little doubt that the *Iliad* and *Odyssey* sprang from traditions that thrived for a long period in a nonliterate culture before they were frozen into a written, relatively fixed form.[2] Of the four mythical bards listed above, Homer is clearly the one for whom the most evidence is available. We have what scholars, ancient and modern, have agreed to be the core of his oeuvre, enough to assess the relationship between the poetry itself and what was said about the poet. We also have many ancient biographies and countless anecdotes (including a contest with Hesiod). But there is no reason to believe a single word contained in all the ancient biographies of Homer. The narrators of the *Iliad* and *Odyssey* speak with indistinguishable voices, telling the audience absolutely nothing about themselves of an autobiographical nature. This composite Homeric speaker (or "persona" on the analogy of the "masks" or "characters" of drama) is anonymous and elusive. His only claim about himself is one that is inseparable from this sort of poetry: He claims access to the tradition of song through the Muses. Of Mousaios we can say very little, for lack of evidence. In the case of Orpheus, however, if the poetry survived intact and narrated in the first person all the beautiful stories—how he charmed the beasts from the mountains and visited the realm of Death to bring back his love—we would have no less hesitation than we do now in saying that this is indeed a fabricated poetic persona, an identity every bit as mythic as what he sings.

And the fourth member of the quartet? Hesiod? Should we believe him when he tells us about himself and his family? What he claims (the Muses' visit aside) is not fantastic or impossible. The background he creates for himself in his song is the opposite of glorious or prestigious. Indeed, there is a striking paradox in his claim to be so humble in his origins, while at the same time he asserts his ability and right to advise kings and sing the generations of the gods. Is this as well a finely articulated and carefully developed posturing of the poetry itself, an individual voice and a character that were first invented by preliterate bards, then manipulated and brought to the form they take in the preserved corpus by the needs of an important cultural institution? On the whole, this explanation, fantastic

---

2. This modern history of this area of research begins with the work of Milman Parry, extended by Albert Lord. See Lord's *Singer of Tales* for an account of it. The relevance of this understanding of the oral roots of Greek hexameter poetry for Hesiod is explored both in Gregory Nagy, "Hesiod," and in Robert Lamberton, *Hesiod*, ch. 1.

as this might seem, is probably more likely than one based on the sudden invention of a personal, confessional (and even truthful) poetic voice by an eighth-century Boeotian peasant.

The Poet of Rural Life

A good deal has already been said above about the dramatic situation that gives the *Works and Days* its shape and texture, unique in archaic Greek poetry. That there is a disjunction between the domestic drama of that situation and the information conveyed must be clear at once. The advice to which the speaker treats his brother Perses is quite disparate, a jumbled collection of myths, proverbs, and farming lore, with a self-sufficient and apparently otherwise irrelevant treatise thrown in at the end, concerned with the problem of choosing the right day of the month for each activity. No one poet could imaginably claim to be the original author of all this material, nor in fact does Hesiod make this claim. Let us not forget that Hesiod (the Hesiod of the *Theogony* prologue, the one who names himself) claimed only that he *was* a shepherd, before he became a poet. He certainly didn't claim to be a practising shepherd at the moment of the performance of his *Theogony*, far from it. From line 36 [35]) onwards ("But why all this about oak tree or stone?"), that poem has nothing to do with peasants, with shepherds who sleep out under the stars, or with anything rustic. It is a poetic theogony that claims as its authority the initiation and inspiration of the Muses. Its speaker has no more developed individuality than the speaker of the *Iliad* or *Odyssey*. He is an inspired poet, a figure of power and authority unqualified by any idiosyncratic characteristics.

The situation in the *Works and Days* is different, but not totally so. This speaker is still in Askra, while the *Theogony* is presumably to be imagined as being performed in a rather grander location. He is embroiled in the day-to-day nastiness of legal squabbles with a good-for-nothing brother, one who now compounds his sins by coming to his more successful brother for a handout. But this poet has already been on the road and come home a success. And that is part of his power over his brother. He claims the right and the ability to sing a wide range of traditional poetry of practical application to various activities that Perses might want or need to engage in. But a good part of this information has explicitly and emphatically *not* been gained from experience. This is a poet who paradoxically insists on his ability to deliver advice on seamanship and maritime matters even though he has gone to sea only once in his life, and that as a passenger on a short crossing. Should we take it that there is an implicit claim to know the rest of his material—planting and harvesting and the rest—from experience? Not at all. The cracker-barrel bard is integrated into his environment by his rural background here, and that poetic identity is brought to bear with a peculiar and attractive appropriateness to practical information on farming. But Hesiod could every bit as easily say, "I'll tell you how to make a plow—though god forbid I should ever have to make one myself." Only a fool learns from experience. Essential to the self-advertisement of this poetic voice is the valuation of the poetic tradition of practical (and theoretical) wisdom *over* the painful groping that characterizes the pitiful and unproductive work of those of us neither so fortunate as to have been taught by the Muses, nor so intelligent as to have listened to the bard who *has*.

We can say with confidence, then, where Hesiod got his information: He learned it from the Muses, which is to say, the poetic tradition, fragmented progeny of Memory. In practical terms, we must assume that the singer whose voice we hear in this poem had a teacher, who had learned the material in turn from his teacher or teachers, and so forth. If this singer's claim to have learned directly from the Muses amounts to a claim to be self-taught (or to have learned the poetic tradition through no human agency), then it can only be a function of the singer's identification with the founder of his line of poetic tradition. This is, in fact, one credible model to explain where the figures of Homer, Hesiod, and the other mythic bards come from. They are projections, founding figures, created by various traditions of oral poetry in order to explain their origins. They are thus capable of evolving with the poetry.

Can we look beyond this tradition of song and identify its debts and sources? We can, but only in the most general terms. What may broadly be called "wisdom literature" is an extremely widespread phenomenon.[3] Books of instruction addressed to princes or simply by fathers to sons are preserved from as early as the third millenium BCE from Sumer and Egypt, and to this day the literatures of traditional societies are rich in advice, often in the form of what we might call "proverbs." That a large part of the material that makes up the *Works and Days* belongs to this genre is clear, but the question of influence is a very complex one. The patterns of behavior that generate such texts are so widespread that they cannot be said to be characteristic of any one culture or group of cultures. The great libraries of Nineveh and Bogazköy contained texts of this sort,

---

3. A very valuable survey of the genre with special reference to the *Works and Days* can be found in M. L. West's edition of the poem, pp. 3–25.

and they contained translations as well, but this is a form of verbal art that belongs only secondarily to libraries, or even to writing, and libraries are unlikely to have served as major channels of influence in its dissemination. The same can be said of quite a lot of the material in the *Works and Days*, notably the beast fable (203 [230]) ff.), a genre of very wide distribution in traditional cultures.

Material culture (pottery, sculpture, architecture, etc.) provides a great deal of evidence of the influence of Egypt and Mesopotamia on the Greeks. In those cultures, literacy stretches back at least a millennium and a half before the limited Greek "Linear B" literacy of the late Bronze Age, and over two millennia before the development of the Greek alphabet. In the Bronze Age, and then again in the archaic period, eastern influences on developing Greek art are evident. That cultural material of a verbal nature moved along the same channels of distribution seems inevitable—after all, one of the major technological advances that the Greeks of the archaic period owed to their neighbors to the east was the alphabet itself, adapted from the Phoenician alphabet not long (we think) before the time the poems of Homer and Hesiod were assembled. The evidence available allows no greater certainty or specificity, but given that poetry resembling Hesiod's existed in the East at a date well before the differentiation of the Greek language itself, and given the demonstrable patterns of influence represented in the archaeological record, the likelihood is very great that Eastern influence, whether in the Bronze Age, in the archaic period, or both, was a necessary prerequisite to the emergence of the earliest Greek poetic traditions.

We may well wonder what practical utility this poetry might have. We have seen that the poem is quite explicit about the practical value it claims for itself. The speaker lectures Perses for his own good, so that he can learn how to get his life together, realize the necessity of work, earn his own livelihood by farming (and even merchant seafaring), learn the proper way to relate to others, and pick the propitious days for a variety of activities. The ultimate goal of all this is prosperity—or at least a level of income that will free Perses from having to go begging to his brother for help. But as we have seen, this lecture is clearly addressed not simply to this mute internal audience, but to an external one. What were they to make of it? Did anyone ever really learn to farm from this poem, or one like it? The questions should be taken separately. I suspect that no one ever learned to farm from this poem in the very elegant, sophisticated, dramatic form in which we have it. This is a performance piece that finds its closest analogies in epic on the one hand, and Athenian drama on the other. Its impact is first and foremost an esthetic impact. This does not mean that the proverbs are not still proverbs and intended to be taken seriously, or the advice on lucky days anything but what it claims. But the account of the farmer's year is memorable for its descriptions of the seasons rather than the practicalities of building a plow. Did anyone ever learn to farm from a poem *like* this one? That is a harder question. The Homeric poems, it has been claimed, constituted an oral encyclopedia— a vast storehouse of the accumulated wisdom of the Greeks, preserving history as well as essential information on how to live and how to act. If Homer was an oral encyclopedist, then it would seem that the Hesiodic poems have an even stronger claim to such status, given their content and explicit aims. The *Works and Days* preserves essential information of a practical nature, packaged in a form that privileges the esthetic and the values of performance. These values are less evident in the lists of prohibitions, the sequences of proverbs, and the closing section on lucky and unlucky days, and in those parts of the poem we seem to have traditional poetry of instruction in essentially raw form, simply collected, and placed in a dramatic frame. Farming lore, including advice on natural indicators of the appropriate dates for seasonal activities, was undoubtedly stored in similar ways, and what we have in the central portion of the *Works and Days* is that material in a richly esthetically enhanced form—not the oral encyclopedia itself, but the coffee-table book at the end of that tradition.

Finally, what use can we make of the poem today? If its constituent parts once had practical pedagogical value, that value is of course long lost. We can, on the one hand, mine the *Works and Days* for evidence of the realities of rural life and the values of archaic Greece.[4] The fact that we are incapable of dating either the poems or their constituent parts with any precision, however, limits their usefulness as evidence. Historians are sometimes reluctant to acknowledge this fact, and simply assign a date (say, 700) and then use the material culture of the period to illuminate the poem, and (to complete the circle) the poem to explain the material culture. What has already been said about the nature of the traditions that produced archaic Greek poetry indicates why one must be very cautious. Any element, any line or formulaic phrase might in fact have its origins much earlier or much later than 700. We have no way of knowing just

---

4.   Hesiod's poetry is often used in this way. See, for example, M. I. Finley, *Early Greece: The Bronze and Archaic Ages*, and Anthony Snodgrass, *Archaic Greece, the Age of Experiment*. Both of these books are very useful for the general historical and cultural context of early Greek poetry.

how closely the poem we have resembles an original from the dawn of Greek literacy or what sort of modification it may have undergone before a stable text was produced, centuries later.

There is, however, one use of the poem that is unimpeachable. I have already suggested that what we have here is the end product of a tradition of wisdom poetry that reaches far back before Greek literacy, one in which esthetic considerations can be seen already displacing earlier functions. That esthetic object is both precious and very accessible. The one-sided conversation between Hesiod and his downtrodden brother is one of the most vivid dramas in the corpus of archaic Greek poetry. It has the wonderful directness of Homeric epic, and if it does not compare with Homer in scale or emotional range, it far surpasses him in wit.

Hesiod the Theologian

In the *Theogony*, Hesiod invented a creative compendium of the theological traditions of archaic Greece. Is this what the Greeks of the seventh century BCE believed about their gods? No. It is what one tradition of poetic theology claimed to be the truth about the generations of the gods. Local cults had their priests, their temples, and their traditions, most of them lost to us, or collected only centuries after Hesiod's *Theogony* was composed. But the larger myths, the stories of the Panhellenic deities, divorced from a specific cult site and its traditions, were the property not of the priests but of the poets.

That is to say that consistency is not to be expected. The myths existed only in the telling, and the rules governing the telling were esthetic rules, their target the imagination. Poetic theologies competed one with another. What Homer says about the generations of the gods is not infrequently at odds with what Hesiod tells us. There was also an Orphic account of the origin of the gods and the universe that was very much at variance with the Hesiodic—in fact, there were several different Orphic accounts, inconsistent in turn with one another. Finally, there were "transitional" figures such as Pherecydes of Syros (traditionally the teacher of Pythagoras, the "first philosopher"). Credited with the invention of prose, Pherecydes created a theogony in mythic language, resembling the Hesiodic account, but manipulating the symbolic deities in a way that anticipates the (generally nonmythic) level of cosmological speculation that we are accustomed to call "philosophical." Hesiod's account was, then, one among many, but its survival, along with the fact that it is so often quoted by later authors, indicates that it did have a certain preeminence among the competitors.

Hesiod's poem is a cosmogony (an account of the origin of the cosmos) of a sort, as well as a theogony, because the deities whose generations are recounted include the major elements of the physical universe: Heaven, Earth, Ocean, and so forth. But it is a cosmogony only secondarily. It is concerned not so much to give an account of where the physical universe came from as to explain where the gods came from, along with the current order in the universe. To put it differently, in creating this cosmos in which Gaia is simultaneously the physical earth and a huge, primal, anthropomorphic deity, Hesiod is generating a human universe and giving an account of the world of our experience.

The poem opens with a very long prologue, a hymn to the Muses that includes an account of Hesiod's encounter with them on Helikon. This is the first extant account of poetic initiation in the European tradition, and it has often been imitated, starting in antiquity. It is in a very real sense the earliest European account of the invention of the poet, and when the Muses tell Hesiod (28–29 [27–28]):

> We know how to tell many believable lies,
> But also, when we want to, how to speak the plain truth

it is clear that the issue of the truth and fiction is addressed here in far more sophisticated terms than in the *Iliad*. Notice that the Muses simply observe that they know both truth and lies. They do not promise to favor Hesiod with the truth.

Hesiod's cosmos begins from a "gaping" or "abyss" (Gk. *khaos*) that simply "was" in the beginning. As we later learn, this abyss still exists: It is what separates Earth from Tartaros below. But if the abyss, the space in between Earth and Tartaros, was the first thing, how could that have existed without Earth and Tartaros, which define its limits? The problem does not emerge, since both of these limiting entities are immediately generated, along with Eros (Desire). Why Eros? Never clearly personified in Homer, Desire is nevertheless associated with Aphrodite later in the *Theogony* (203 [201]) and later poets make Eros Aphrodite's child. To place this principle at the beginning of things, only to subordinate it to Aphrodite later, is a decision that suggests complex motives in this theogony. Eros is needed at the beginning of the generation of the gods (and the universe) because desire, the erotic principle, brings about all the couplings that follow, to produce the world as we know it. However rudimentary, this is a statement that looks more philosophical than religious, in that it posits a kind of *first principle* (albeit represented in the form of a deity) as the force that gets things going.

The remainder of the poem is a similar mixture of what appears to be inherited lore and what appears to be invention, or explanation, in the form of creative mythmaking. A number of examples are indicated in the notes below. A striking one that occurs in the prologue is the presentation of those especially Hesiodic deities, the Muses, who probably receive their names for the first time here, names that designate in various ways the capacity to give a pleasure that is primarily, but not exclusively, esthetic.

The heart of the *Theogony* is a succession myth that explains the background of the current cosmic order: the rule of the Olympian gods under the leadership of Zeus. There are two major stages in this succession. Earth's first child, Ouranos, becomes her consort and the first dominant male deity of the succession myth. Gaia produces other offspring parthenogenetically, without Ouranos' help, and the monster Typhaon is fathered on her by Tartaros, but the core of the next generation, children of Heaven and Earth, are the twelve Titans. The relationships between sexual partners and between fathers and progeny in these primitive generations are exceptionally vicious and violent. If this is Eros at work, no one would ever confuse him with "love." Ouranos simply stuffed the Titans (and then the Cyclopes and Hundred-handers) back inside their mother, because, as Hesiod tells us, he "feared and loathed" them (156 [155]). The youngest of this first generation of Titans, Kronos, resolves this painful situation for his mother by removing his father's reproductive capacity in the most direct way: He reaches out from whichever recess of Earth we choose to imagine him confined in, and castrates his father as he settles onto Gaia. The blood generates more deities as it falls on Earth, and Aphrodite emerges from the severed genitals, floating in the sea.

Lists of the offspring of Night and Sea (Pontos) follow, before the poem returns to the central thread of the succession myth at 341(337). The offspring of the Titans are recounted in the central portion of the poem, which extends all the way to 618 (617), with increasingly lengthy narrative expansions, including the birth of Zeus and the longer version of the Prometheus story, also told in the *Works and Days*. Kronos as the victor over Ouranos becomes his successor, and his solution to the problem of progeny is closely parallel to that of his father. Instead of shoving them back inside their mother, he swallows them himself, until Gaia and Rheia plot together to hide Zeus from him, substituting a stone. In a manner not disclosed, Zeus then liberates his siblings, and also his uncles the Centaurs (502 [501]) and finally the Hundred-handers (629 [626]). The second succession to the rule of the universe is accomplished not by castration but by military takeover. The Hundred-handers give him a crucial edge, and Zeus leads the Olympians to victory over the Titans and confines them in Tartaros. This provides the context for a description of Tartaros (724–812 [724–806]). After Zeus has overcome the final challenge of Typhaon and distributed the honors to the victorious Olympians, the poem turns to his various wives and offspring and a few other couplings of Olympians to fill out the traditional Olympian pantheon. At 973 (963), the narrator abruptly shifts from the matings among the Olympians to those of goddesses with mortal men, a prelude to the final transition, at the end of the poem, to the (lost) *Catalogue of Women*.

The *Theogony*, then, is a huge prologue to what may well be the oldest of all this material, the catalogue of the women of the heroic age. This helps to put the material in perspective. One function of all this poetry about the Bronze Age, produced in the context of archaic, Iron Age Greece, was the legitimation of the powerful families that traced their origins back to the heroes and, eventually, to the gods. The matings of the deities that generate the universe as we know it and its order are the prologue to the matings that explain the patterns of power and prestige in the world of men.

We were able to point only vaguely to the sources of the disparate material in the *Works and Days*. Here, we can be more specific about the nature of Greek theology's debts to Mesopotamia. In the cities between the rivers, king lists organized human history, and these lists themselves, at a sufficient distance in time, merged into god lists. The projection of human power onto the divine plane provided the pattern, and the conception of the universe as itself a city with a succession of rulers was a natural product of this process. Succession myths exist in other cultures, independent of the developments in Egypt and Mesopotamia, but in this instance we can follow the diffusion of the concept. The Hittite succession myth is dependent on Semitic prototypes that passed on westward to the Greeks. The Hittites themselves may have had some role as intermediaries, but this was hardly needed, since direct contacts with the east can easily be documented for the Greek world back into the Bronze Age.

Those two lines at the end of the *Theogony* as we have it, in which the poet builds the bridge to the next poem, alter in retrospect everything that has gone before. Epic poems, we know, were in fact strung together. A medieval marginal note preserves the evidence that some ancient copies of the *Iliad* ended with a similar bridge to the next poem in the narrative of the Trojan War, the *Aithioipis*. Such bridge passages may in fact have had a considerable influence on claims about authorship of the poems in the sequences. And it may be that there is some special appropriateness in placing theogonies in front of other poems, as prologues. It would seem, in any case, that in some strange sense the succession of the Hesiodic poems echoed those Mesopotamian king lists, trailing back into lists of gods. The Mesopotamian lists and the Greek poetry seem to have served similar functions in accounting for order and hierarchy, present and past, in and out of time.

For us, the *Theogony* is important primarily because it is our greatest single archaic Greek compendium of myths about the gods. We have seen that it is idiosyncratic and that no such book could have been definitive or authoritative in its time. Despite wonderful passages, and poetry that relishes effects so extreme that they run the risk of becoming grotesque, the *Theogony* does not have the esthetic coherence or the wit of the *Works and Days*. That poem, along with the opening lines of the *Theogony* prologue, accomplished something that was to change archaic Greek poetry in a fundamental way, by personalizing the speaking voice and inventing a narrator with an identity and a personality. If there is a single achievement of the poetry that reaches us under Hesiod's name that stands out over all the others, it is that: the invention of the poet.

BIBLIOGRAPHY

The most important books for any reader of the *Theogony* and *Works and Days* must inevitably be M. L. West's editions of the Greek text of the two poems:

Hesiod, *Theogony*, edited with prolegomena and commentary by M. L. West. Oxford: Oxford University Press, 1966.
Hesiod, *Works and Days*, edited with prolegomena and commentary by M. L. West. Oxford: Oxford University Press, 1978.

It might seem odd to suggest such books to readers of an English translation, but their editor has spent more time with the myriad problems in the text and ideas of the Hesiodic poems than anyone else alive, and his voluminous commentaries make that work richly available. There is hardly a word in these poems that is not in some sense problematic. If you cannot go to the Greek, the next best thing is to go as close as you can and to read the poems over M. L. West's shoulder.

For a broader overview, see either Gregory Nagy, "Hesiod" in *Ancient Authors*, ed. T. J. Luce, New York: Scribner's (1982) or Robert Lamberton, *Hesiod*, Hermes Books, New Haven: Yale University Press (1988). Both of the above will supply further bibliography. For an account of the oral poetic traditions relevant to the ancient Greeks, see Albert B. Lord, *The Singer of Tales*, New York: Atheneum (1964).

Finally, for historical reconstructions of the age that produced these poems, see M. I. Finley, *Early Greece: The Bronze and Archaic Ages*, Ancient Culture and Society, London: Chatto and Windus (2nd. ed., 1981) and Anthony Snodgrass, *Archaic Greece, The Age of Experiment* London: Dent (1980).

TRANSLATOR'S PREFACE

The poet Jared Carter compares the art of oral poetry practiced by Hesiod to the art of early New Orleans jazz musicians, live performers who played not by rote but by heart, improvising from their common store of melodies, riffs, and chord changes, developing out of the shared tradition their personal styles, and transmitting the art to the next generation.[1] This is a wonderfully apt comparison for what it suggests about the poetic process in archaic Greece. Hesiod composed without writing, in a tradition of oral composition and performance whose origins are lost to us but which has parallels in Vedic and other ancient cultures. We might call the particular tradition that Hesiod worked in the Helikonian School of Practical Poetics, after the Muse-haunted mountain, Helikon, where there were poetry and music festivals and where Hesiod learned and practiced his art. Hesiod in fact may have been more a school of poetry than a person. In any case, Hesiodic poetry has a definite local flavor to it, a personal landscape behind it, and a personal voice within it that is quite unlike the vast epic canvas and almost disembodied voice of his near-contemporary Homer. Hesiod's poetry is different from Homeric heroic narrative also in that it really is practical, specializing in lore of all kinds—agricultural, religious, nautical, moral—a poetic practice whose raw material is lists, calendars, maxims, genealogies, fables, prayers, myths, diatribes, and personal reminiscences. This is poetry that codifies and transmits cultural knowledge, didactic poetry as it is sometimes called, but poetry nonetheless, eloquence as a mode of song.

The rhythmic line that underlies Greek didactic poetry is the dactylic hexameter, the same line used in epic—six long syllabic pulses, each one followed by two light syllables or a single unstressed long syllable. It is a supple line, capable of a wide range of modulation and effects, with attention to where pauses are situated within the line. Words and phrases, especially epithets, of certain rhythmic shapes tended to be used and reused in certain parts of the line, and entire lines or short sequences of lines describing recurrent activities tended to be reused. These formulas, as they are called, were part of the shared tradition. They served as aids for composition and performance, but they are also an important part of the poem's esthetic signature, in both respects not unlike riffs in jazz.

1. Jared Carter, "Hesiod: Poet and Peasant Overtures," *Chicago Review*, Winter, 1990.

Other stylistic devices cover the entire range of tropes, all the figures of
sense and of sound (except end-rhyme, which is not a feature of ancient
Greek poetry) familiar to all students of poetry, elements of an art already
well developed by the time Hesiod received it.

   Hesiod's oral poems eventually were transcribed and became poetic
texts, and it is as texts that the translator encounters and transmits them.
Translation, however it might transform a text, is by nature a conservative
process, an act of conservation; and this translation of Hesiod accounts
for every line and every word in M. L. West's Oxford editions (Greek
line numbers are given in brackets in the notes). But it is not a line-by-
line, word-for-word translation, an approach that would be incompatible
with the larger project of getting at the ground sense of Hesiod's poetry.
Rhythmically, this translation moves more in anapests (short-short-long)
than the Greek's dactyls (which have never been naturalized in English),
preserving something of the triple-time movement of the original and at
the same time setting up speech cadences that help establish the persona.
Verse and sentence rhythms are often more effective than dialect in
suggesting a regional tone, and that is the strategy here. Hesiod's own
dialect was the standard epic Ionic that Homer also used, with a slightly
higher proportion of Aeolicisms, perhaps echoing his father's origins.
The regional cast of the translation, especially in *Works and Days*,
might be described as south-central midland, the language of much of
America's small rural towns. The occasional use of rhyme and broken
rhyme in some of the mnemonic verses in *Works and Days* does not
reflect any Greek usage but is meant to suggest the traditional wisdom of
preexistent proverbs. The text is arranged on the page in ways that have
little to do with oral poetry or Greek manuscript tradition but much to
do with the rhetorical shape and structure of the poems. Section titles
are added in the same spirit. All of this is in aid of what, along with
philological accuracy, is the main goal of the translation: recreating
in American English the poetic voice that is chartered in *Theogony*
and sounds through *Works and Days*, a plain, rural voice that rises to
passionate eloquence enunciating the themes of the justice of Zeus, the
hard lot of humans, and the redemptive value of poetry.

I would like to thank William Levitan for an early critical reading of the
translation, as well as Donald Allen, Beth Bailey, Anne Carson, Donald
Carne-Ross, Guy Davenport, Jim Hartman, Douglass Parker, and Donald
Sheehan for their comments. An award from the Translation Center at
Columbia University helped support the work. Besides providing the

introduction and notes, Robert Lamberton served as Hackett's reader and pointed out many details in need of revision. I consulted Kathleen Whalen in making these revisions. James Silver helped compile the glossary, and Linda Montgomery helped with everything at the end. My thanks to all of them; to numerous students who have worked on Hesiod with me through the years; to my wife, Judy Roitman, for her critical advice and constant support; and to my son, Ben, and my daughter, Ursula, who listened to me tell Hesiod's stories. I am grateful to have Anne Carson's art on the cover. The translations are dedicated to my father, Peter Lombardo, a craftsman who also worked the soil, and who was a good and just man.

Stanley Lombardo
University of Kansas

WORKS & DAYS

Muses of the sacred spring Pieria
Who give glory in song,
Come sing Zeus' praises, hymn your great Father
Through whom mortals are either
Renowned or unknown, famous or unfamed   5
As goes the will of great Zeus.
Easy for Him to build up the strong
And tear the strong down.
Easy for Him to diminish the mighty
And magnify the obscure.   10
Easy for Him to straighten the crooked
And wither the proud,

Zeus the Thunderer
Whose house is most high.

Bend hither your mind,   15
Hand down just judgments,
O Thou!

And as for me,
Well, brother Perses,
I'd like to state a few facts.   20

Two Kinds of Strife

It looks like there's not just one kind of Strife—
That's Eris—after all, but two on the Earth.
You'd praise one of them once you got to know her,
But the other's plain blameworthy. They've just got
Completely opposite temperaments.   25
One of them favors war and fighting. She's a mean cuss
And nobody likes her, but everybody honors her,
This ornery Eris. They have to: it's the gods' will.

The other was born first though. Ebony Night
30   Bore her, and Kronos' son who sits high in thin air
Set her in Earth's roots, and she's a lot better for humans.
Even shiftless folks she gets stirred up to work.

When a person's lazing about and sees his neighbor
Getting rich, because he hurries to plow and plant
35   And put his homestead in order, he tends to compete
With that neighbor in a race to get rich.

> Strife like this does people good.

> So potter feuds with potter
> And carpenter with carpenter,
40   Beggar is jealous of beggar
> And poet of poet.

Now, Perses, you lay these things up in your heart
And don't let the mischief-loving Eris keep you from work,
Spending all your time in the market eyeballing quarrels
45   And listening to lawsuits. A person hasn't any business
Wasting time at the market unless he's got a year's supply
Of food put by, grain from Demeter out of the ground.
When you've got plenty of that, you can start squabbling
Over other people's money.
50   Not that you're going to get
Another chance with me. Let's settle this feud right now
With the best kind of judgment, a straight one from Zeus.
We had our inheritance all divided up, then you
Made off with most of it, playing up to those
55   Bribe-eating lords who love cases like this.
Damn fools. Don't know the half from the whole,
Or the real goodness in mallows and asphodel.

Why Life Is Hard

You know, the gods never have let on
How humans might make a living. Else,
60   You might get enough done in one day
To keep you fixed for a year without working.

You might just hang your plowshare up in the smoke,
And all the fieldwork done by your oxen
And hard-working mules would soon run to ruin.
But Zeus got his spleen up, and went and hid   *65*
How to make a living, all because shifty Prometheus
Tricked him. That's why Zeus made life hard for humans.
He hid fire. But that fine son of Iapetos stole it
Right back out from under Zeus' nose, hiding
The flame in a fennel stalk. And thundering Zeus   *70*
Who rides herd on the clouds got angry and said:

"Iapetos' boy, if you're not the smartest of them all!
I bet you're glad you stole fire and outfoxed me.
But things will go hard for you and for humans after this.
I'm going to give them Evil in exchange for fire,   *75*
Their very own Evil to love and embrace."

That's what he said, the Father of gods and men,
And he laughed out loud. Then he called Hephaistos
And told him to hurry and knead some earth and water
And put a human voice in it, and some strength,   *80*
And to make the face like an immortal goddess' face
And the figure like a beautiful, desirable virgin's.
Then he told Athene to teach her embroidery & weaving,
And Aphrodite golden to spill grace on her head
And painful desire and knee-weakening anguish.   *85*
And he ordered the quicksilver messenger, Hermes,
To give her a bitchy mind and a cheating heart.
That's what he told them, and they listened to Lord Zeus,
Kronos' son. And right away famous old Gimpy
Plastered up some clay to look like a shy virgin   *90*
Just like Zeus wanted, and the Owl-Eyed Goddess
Got her all dressed up, and the Graces divine
And Lady Persuasion put some gold necklaces
On her skin, and the Seasons (with their long, fine hair)
Put on her head a crown of springtime flowers.   *95*
Pallas Athena put on the finishing touches,
And the quicksilver messenger put in her breast
Lies and wheedling words and a cheating heart,
Just like rumbling Zeus wanted. And the gods' own herald

100   Put a voice in her, and he named that woman
      Pandora, because all the Olympians donated something,
      And she was a real pain for human beings.

      When this piece of irresistible bait was finished,
      Zeus sent Hermes to take her to Epimetheus
105   As a present, and the speedy messenger-god did it.
      Epimetheus didn't think on what Prometheus had told him,
      Not to accept presents from Olympian Zeus but to send any
      Right back, in case trouble should come of it to mortals.
      No, Epimetheus took it, and after he had the trouble
110   Then he thought on it.
                            Because before that the human race
      Had lived off the land without any trouble, no hard work,
      No sickness or pain that the Fates give to men
      (And when men are in misery they show their age quickly).
115   But the woman took the lid off the big jar with her hands
      And scattered all the miseries that spell sorrow for men.
      Only Hope was left there in the unbreakable container,
      Stuck under the lip of the jar, and couldn't fly out:
      The woman clamped the lid back on the jar first,
120   All by the plan of the Aegisholder, cloud-herding Zeus.
      But ten thousand or so other horrors spread out among men,
      The earth is full of evil things, and so's the sea.
      Diseases wander around just as they please, by day and by night,
      Soundlessly, since Zeus in his wisdom deprived them of voice.
125   There's just no way you can get around the mind of Zeus.

      If you want, I can sum up another tale for you,
      Neat as you please. The main point to remember
      Is that gods and humans go back a long way together.

The Five Ages

      Golden was the first race of articulate folk
130   Created by the immortals who live on Olympos.
      They actually lived when Kronos was king of the sky,
      And they lived like gods, not a care in their hearts,
      Nothing to do with hard work or grief,
      And miserable old age didn't exist for them.

From fingers to toes they never grew old,   *135*
And the good times rolled. And when they died
It was like sleep just ravelled them up.
They had everything good. The land bore them fruit
All on its own, and plenty of it too. Cheerful folk,
They did their work peaceably and in prosperity,   *140*
With plenty of flocks, and they were dear to the gods.
And sure when Earth covered over that generation
They turned into holy spirits, powers above ground,
Invisible wardens for the whole human race.
They roam all over the land, shrouded in mist,   *145*
Tending to justice, repaying criminal acts
And dispensing wealth. This is their royal honor.

Later, the Olympians made a second generation,
Silver this time, not nearly so fine as the first,
Not at all like the gold in either body or mind.   *150*
A child would be reared at his mother's side
A hundred years, just a big baby, playing at home.
And when they finally did grow up and come of age
They didn't live very long, and in pain at that,
Because of their lack of wits. They just could not stop   *155*
Hurting each other and could not bring themselves
To serve the Immortals, nor sacrifice at their altars
The way men ought to, wherever and whenever. So Zeus,
Kronos' son, got angry and did away with them
Because they weren't giving the Blessed Gods their honors.   *160*

And when Earth had covered over that generation—
Blessed underground mortals is what they are called,
Second in status, but still they have their honor—
Father Zeus created a third generation
Of articulate folk, **Bronze** this time, not like   *165*
The silver at all, made them out of ash trees,
Kind of monstrous and heavy, and all they cared about
Was fighting and war. They didn't eat any food at all.
They had this kind of hard, untameable spirit.
Shapeless hulks. Terrifically strong. Grapplehook hands   *170*
Grew out of their shoulders on thick stumps of arms,
And they had bronze weapons, bronze houses,

And their tools were bronze. No black iron back then.
Finally they killed each other off with their own hands
175   And went down into the bone-chilling halls of Hades
And left no names behind. Astounding as they were,
Black Death took them anyway, and they left the sun's light.

So Earth buried that generation too,
And Zeus fashioned a fourth race
180   To live off the land, juster and nobler,
The divine race of **Heroes**, also called
Demigods, the race before the present one.
They all died fighting in the great wars,
Some at seven-gated Thebes, Kadmos' land,
185   In the struggle for Oidipous' cattle,
And some, crossing the water in ships,
Died at Troy, for the sake of beautiful Helen.
And when Death's veil had covered them over
Zeus granted them a life apart from other men,
190   Settling them at the ends of the Earth.
And there they live, free from all care,
In the Isles of the Blest, by Ocean's deep stream,
Blessed heroes for whom the life-giving Earth
Bears sweet fruit ripening three times a year.

195   [Far from the Immortals, and Kronos is their king,
For the Father of gods and men has released him
And he still has among them the honor he deserves.
Then the fifth generation: Broad-browed Zeus
Made still another race of articulate folk
200   To people the plentiful Earth.]
                                                            I wish
I had nothing to do with this fifth generation,
Wish I had died before or been born after,

Because this is the **Iron Age.**
205   Not a day goes by
A man doesn't have some kind of trouble.
Nights too, just wearing him down. I mean
The gods send us terrible pain and vexation.
Still, there'll be some good mixed in with the evil,

And then Zeus will destroy this generation too,   *210*
Soon as they start being born grey around the temples.
Then fathers won't get along with their kids anymore,
Nor guests with hosts, nor partner with partner,
And brothers won't be friends, the way they used to be.
Nobody'll honor their parents when they get old   *215*
But they'll curse them and give them a hard time,
Godless rascals, and never think about paying them back
For all the trouble it was to raise them.
They'll start taking justice into their own hands,
Sacking each other's cities, no respect at all   *220*
For the man who keeps his oaths, the good man,
The just man. No, they'll keep all their praise
For the wrongdoer, the man who is violence incarnate,
And shame and justice will lie in their hands.
Some good-for-nothing will hurt a decent man   *225*
Slander him, and swear an oath on top of it.
Envy will be everybody's constant companion,
With her foul mouth and hateful face, relishing evil.
And then
                        up to Olympos from the wide-pathed Earth,   *230*
                        lovely apparitions wrapped in white veils,
                        off to join the Immortals, abandoning humans
There go **Shame** and **Nemesis**. And horrible suffering
Will be left for mortal men, and no defense against evil.

And here's a fable for kings, who'll not need it explained: *235*

It's what the hawk said high in the clouds
As he carried off a speckle-throated nightingale
Skewered on his talons. She complained something pitiful,
And he made this high and mighty speech to her:
"No sense in your crying. You're in the grip of real strength now,   *240*
And you'll go where I take you, songbird or not.
I'll make a meal of you if I want, or I might let you go.
Only a fool struggles against his superiors.
He not only gets beat, but humiliated as well."

Thus spoke the hawk, the windlord, his long wings beating.   *245*

Justice

But you, Perses, you listen to Justice
And don't cultivate Violence.
                              Violent behavior is bad
For a poor man. Even a rich man can't afford it
250   But it's going to bog him down in Ruin some day.
There's a better road around the other way
Leading to what's right. When it comes down to it
Justice beats out Violence. A fool learns this the hard way.
Also, Oath, who's a god, keeps up with crooked verdicts,
255   And there's a ruckus when the Lady Justice
Gets dragged through the streets by corrupt judges
Who swallow bribes and pervert their verdicts.
Later, she finds her way back into town, weeping,
Wrapped in mist, and she gives grief to the men
260   Who drove her out and didn't do right by her.

But when judges judge straight, for neighbors
As well as for strangers, and never turn their backs
On Justice, their city blossoms, their people bloom.
You'll find peace all up and down the land
265   And youngsters growing tall, because broad-browed Zeus
Hasn't marked them out for war. Nor do famine or blight
Ever afflict folk who deal squarely with each other.
They feast on the fruits of their tended fields,
And the earth bears them a good living too.
270   Mountain oaks yield them acorns at the crown,
Bees and honey from the trunk. Their sheep
Are hefty with fleece, and women bear children
Who look like their parents. In short, they thrive
On all the good things life has to offer, and they
275   Never travel on ships. The soil's their whole life.

But for those who live for violence and vice,
Zeus, Son of Kronos, broad-browed god, decrees
A just penalty, and often a whole city suffers
For one bad man and his damn fool schemes.
280   The Son of Kronos sends them disaster from heaven,
Famine and plague, and the folk wither away,

Women stop bearing children, whole families
Die off, by Zeus' Olympian will. Or another time
He might lay low their army, or tumble down
Their city's walls, or sink all their ships at sea.   *285*

Rulers and Lords! It's up to you
To observe this justice. There are, you know,
Immortal beings abroad in this world
Who do observe with what corruption and fraud
Men grind down their neighbors and destroy the state,   *290*
As if they'd never *heard* of angry gods.
Thirty thousand spirits there are on this earth
In the service of Zeus, watching the human race,
Overseeing trials for criminal acts. Invisible,
They roam all through the land, cloaked in mist.   *295*
And there's the Virgin Justice, Zeus' own daughter,
Honored and revered among the Olympian gods.
Whenever anyone hurts her by besmirching her name,
She sits down by the Son of Kronos, her father,
And speaks to him about men's unjust hearts   *300*
Until the people pay for their foolhardy rulers'
Unjust verdicts and biased decisions.
Guard against this, you bribe-eating lords.
Judge rightly. Forget your crooked deals.

Plan harm for another and harm yourself most,   *305*
The evil we hatch always comes home to roost.

The eye of Zeus sees all and knows all,
And, if he wants, he's looking here right now,
And the kind of justice this city harbors
Doesn't fool him one bit. As for me, I'd as soon   *310*
Not be a just man, not myself or my son.
It's no good at all for a man to be just
When the unjust man gets more than what's just.
But I don't look for Zeus in his wisdom
To bring things to that pass for a long time yet.   *315*

Perses, you take all this to heart. Listen
To what's right, and forget about violence.

The Son of Kronos has laid down the law for humans.
Fish and beasts and birds of prey feed on
320   Each other, since there's no justice among them.

But to men he gave justice, and that works out
All to the good. If you know in your heart what's right
And come out and say so, broad-browed Zeus will
Give you prosperity. But if you bear false witness
325   Or lie under oath, and by damaging Justice
Ruin yourself beyond hope of cure, your bloodline
Will weaken and your descendants fade out. But a man
Who stands by his word leaves a strong line of kinfolk.

Now I'm speaking sense to you, Perses you fool.
330   It's easy to get all of Wickedness you want.
She lives just down the road a piece, and it's a smooth road too.
But the gods put Goodness where we have to sweat
To get at her. It's a long, uphill pull
And rough going at first. But once you reach the top
335   She's as easy to have as she was hard at first.

Best of all is the man who sees everything for himself,
Who looks ahead and sees what will be better in the end.
It's a good man too who knows how to take good advice.
But the man who can't see for himself nor take advice,
340   Now that kind of man is a real good-for-nothing.
So at least *listen*, Perses—you come from good stock—
And remember always to work. Work so Hunger'll
Hate you, and Demeter, the venerable crowned goddess,
Will smile on you and fill your barn with food.

345   Hunger is the lazy man's constant companion.
Gods hate him, and men do too, the loafer
Who lives like the stingless drones, wasting
The hive's honey without working themselves,
Eating free.
350   You've got to *schedule* your work
So your sheds will stay full of each season's harvest.
It's work that makes men rich in flocks and goods.
When you work you're a lot dearer to the gods

And to people too. Everybody hates a lay-about.
Work's no disgrace; it's idleness that's a disgrace.   *355*

If you work, the lay-abouts will soon be envying you
Getting rich.
                        With wealth comes honor and glory.
No matter your situation, it's better to work,
Better for you too, Perses, if you'd only   *360*
Get your mind off of other folks' property
And work at earning a living, as I keep telling you.

Shame is sometimes a blessing, sometimes a curse.
Shame, the bad kind, is the poor man's companion.
Shame for the poor, assurance for the rich.   *365*

Wealth's better not grabbed but given by the gods.
If a man lays hold of wealth by main force
Or if he pirates it with his tongue, as happens
All too often when greed hoodwinks a man's sense
And decency gets crowded out by its opposite,   *370*
The gods whittle him down just like that, shrink
His household, and he doesn't stay rich for long.
It's the same thing when somebody wrongs a suppliant
Or a guest, or gets into his brother's bed
And does with his sister-in-law what just isn't right,   *375*
Or like a damn fool wrongs an orphan
Or raises his voice to his old pappy, using
Harsh language with him when he's at death's door.
Zeus himself gets angry with a man like that
And in the end makes him pay for his wrongful acts.   *380*

But you keep your foolish heart away from such behavior,
And, according to your means, sacrifice to the gods,
Observing ritual purity when you burn the fat thighbones,
And on occasion appease them with libations and incense
Both before you sleep and when the holy light returns,   *385*
So may they bless you from propitious hearts, and you
Buy up other folks' farms instead of them buying yours.

Invite your friend to a feast, leave your enemy alone,

And be sure to invite the fellow who lives close by.
390   If you've got some kind of emergency on your hands,
      Neighbors come lickety-split, kinfolk take a while.
      A bad neighbor's as much a curse as a good one's a blessing.
      You've got a real prize if you've got a good neighbor.
      Nary an ox would be lost if it weren't for bad neighbors.
395   Get good measure from a neighbor and give back as good,
      Measure for measure, or better if you're able,
      So when you need something later you can count on him then.

      Don't make dirty money; dirty money spells doomsday.
      Return a friend's friendship and a visitor's visit.
400   Give gifts to the giver, give none to the non-giver.
      The giver gets gifts, the non-giver gets naught.
      And Give's a good girl, but Gimmee's a goblin.
      The man who gives willingly, even if it costs him,
      Takes joy in his giving and is glad in his heart.

405   But let a man turn greedy and grab for himself
      Even something small, it'll freeze his heart stiff.

      It's the saver staves off feverish starvation.
      If you put away a little each day
      Even that little will soon be a lot.

410   What's laid up at home doesn't worry a man.

      Home's best for a body. It's a dangerous world.

      It's great to help yourself from stores on hand
      And a pain in the neck to need what's not there.

      When a jar's full or near empty enjoy all you want.
415   Go easy in between. It's cheap to nurse the dregs.

      Let the wages for a friend be settled on and fixed,
      Even if he's your brother. You can shake hands and smile,
      But get a witness. Trust and mistrust both ruin men.

      Don't let a sashaying female pull the wool over your eyes

With her flirtatious lies. She's fishing for your barn.   *420*
Trust a woman and you'd as well trust a thief.

There should be only one son to support
The father's house. That's the way a family's wealth grows.
Die old if you leave a second son in the house.
Still, Zeus can easily supply plenty all around,   *425*
And more hands mean more help, and a bigger yield.

And if the spirit within you moves you to get rich,
Do as follows:

> *Work, work,* and then *work* some more.

The Farmer's Year

Pleiades rising in the dawning sky,   *430*
   Harvest is nigh.
Pleiades setting in the waning night,
   Plowing is right.
Forty days and nights in the turning year
   They disappear.   *435*
When they shine again in the morning shade,
   Sharpen your blade.

This is the rule for plains & for seabord
And for mountain valleys far from the sea:

Plant naked, plow naked, & reap naked   *440*

If you want to garner all of Demeter's bounty
In season, and have each crop grow when it's due.

That way you won't ever lack and have to beg
At other folks' houses, and get nothing by it.
The way you came to me just now. Well,   *445*
I'm not going to give you another drop.
Work, you fool Perses. Work
The work the gods laid out for men,
Or you'll eat your heart out, you

450   And your wife and kids, looking for a living
      With your neighbors, who couldn't care less.
      Two or three times you might get away with it,
      But if you keep making a nuisance of yourself
      You won't get a thing, and all your big talk
455   Will be useless, a huge waste of words.
      What you've got to do, Perses,
      Is get out of debt and keep from starving.

      First, get yourself a house, a woman, & a plow-ox
      (A slave woman, not for marrying, one who can plow)
460   And stock the house with everything you'll need
      So you won't have to borrow, get turned down, go without,
      And have the season slip by without anything getting done.
      Don't put things off till tomorrow and the next day.
      A man who sloughs off work doesn't fill his barn,
465   Nor does a procrastinator. Keeping at it gets the job done.
      The procrastinator is always wrestling with ruin.

Summer

      When the blistering sun eases its scorching heat
      And the autumn rains come from Zeus almighty
      And a body feels lighter because the Dog Star Sirius
470   Doesn't beat down on our poor doomed heads
      So much by day, but shines more in the night,
      That's the time wood you cut with your axe
      Is least full of wormholes, when the yellow leaves
      Are on the ground, and no new leaves are sprouting.

475   Remember, it's seasonable work to cut your timber then.
      Cut a three-foot mortar and a three-cubit pestle
      And an axle seven-foot. That's the best way to piece it.
      But if you make it eight-foot, you can cut a clod-buster too.
      For a wagon ten palms wide, cut a felly three spans across.
480   Lots of curved pieces too. Search mountain and field
      For a piece the right shape to bring home for a plough-tree,
      Holm-oak, because that's the strongest for oxen
      To plow with, once a craftsman blessed by Athena
      Has fixed in the share and pegged it to the pole.

You really need two plows, and they can both be homemade,   *485*
One jointed and one a solid piece. It's better that way:
If you break one you can hitch your team to the spare.
Poles of laurel or elm are least likely to worm.
Oak's best for the share, holm-oak for the plough-tree.

As for your oxen, get yourself a pair of bulls   *490*
Nine years old: their strength won't be spent yet
And they'll be in their prime, at the best age for work.
Won't fight in the furrow, break the plow
And leave the work unfinished. You'll want a good man of forty
To follow behind. See he has a square meal before work,   *495*
Someone who'll tend to his job and drive a straight furrow,
Too old to be making faces at his friends, a man who'll keep
His mind on his work. Younger than forty, he won't be so good
When it comes to sowing and not oversowing.
A younger man'll be squirming to horse around with his friends.   *500*

Autumn

Mind now, when you hear the call of the crane
Coming from the clouds, as it does year by year:
That's the sign for plowing, and the onset of winter
And the rainy season. That cry bites the heart
Of the man with no ox.   *505*
                Time then to feed your oxen
In their stall. You know it's easy to say,
"Loan me a wagon and a team of oxen."
And it's easy to answer, "Got work for my oxen."
It takes a good imagination for a man to think   *510*
He'll just peg together a wagon. Damn fool,
Doesn't realize there's a hundred timbers make up a wagon
And you have to have 'em laid up beforehand at home.

Soon as you get the first signs for plowing
Get a move on, yourself and your workers,   *515*
And plow straight through wet weather and dry,
Getting a good start at dawn, so your fields
Will fill up. Work the land in spring, too,
But fallow turned in summer won't let you down.

520 Sow your fallow land while the soil's still light.
       Fallow's the charm that keeps wee-uns well-fed.

       Pray to Zeus-in-the-ground and to Demeter sacred
       For Demeter's holy grain to grow thick and full.
       Pray when you first start plowing, when you
525 Take hold of the handle and come down with your stick
       On the backs of the oxen straining at the yoke-pins.
       A little behind, have a slave follow with a hoe
       To make trouble for the birds by covering the seeds.

       Doing things right is the best thing in the world,
530   *Just like doing 'em wrong is the absolute worst.*

       This way you'll have ears of grain bending
       Clear to the ground, *if* the Olympian comes through
       At the end, and you'll be clearing the cobwebs
       Out of your bins, and I hope to tell you
535 You'll be glad to dip into your stores, well-supplied
       Till grey spring comes. No need to look to others:
       Other folks are going to have need of you.

       Plow the shiny soil at the winter solstice though
       And you'll squat to harvest, clutching
540 Thin grain, binding it with ears at both ends,
       Dusty and unhappy, and carry it home
       In a basket, a sorry sight for your neighbors.
       Still, the mind of Zeus the Storm King
       Is hard to predict, variable, changeable.
545 If you do plow late, there might be this cure:
       When the first cuckoo sings in the oak leaves,
       Making men happy the world over, if Zeus
       Makes it rain on the third day and doesn't let up
       Until the water just fills an ox's hoofprint,
550 Then the late plower might do as well as the early.

       Keep all this in mind, and don't let grey spring
       Slip by unnoticed, nor the rainy season either.

Winter

Pass right by the smithy's warm bench
In wintertime, when the cold keeps a man
From outdoor work. Plenty to keep you busy 555
Around the house. Idleness in bad weather
Can pinch you till you're poor, and you're left
Squeezing a thick foot with a thin hand.
A man out of work, a man with empty hopes
And no livelihood, has a mind that runs to mischief. 560
It's a no good kind of hope comes to a man who's broke
Sitting in the blacksmith's with no sure living.
So tell your workers while it's still midsummer:
"It won't always be summer, start building your sheds."

The month of Lenaion, bad days, all of 'em, 565
Take the skin off an ox. Got to protect yourself then
From the hard frosts that form when Boreas blows.
That wind whips on down from the horse-country in Thrace,
Churning up the sea and making the woodlands moan.
Oaks with high crowns up in the valleys, thick firs, 570
It hammers them down to the rich mountain earth
And the whole forest roars. Wild animals shiver
And tuck their tails under, even those with hides
All shadowy with fur, it doesn't matter: that wind's
Cold and blows right through the shaggiest coat. 575
Blows right through oxhide, oxhide won't stop it,
And it'll blow right through a goat's long hair.
Not through sheepskin though, fleece is too thick.
It'll double an old man over like a wagon wheel,
But it can't get through the soft skin of a girl 580
Indoors with her mother, a girl who hasn't yet learned
About Aphrodite golden. She bathes her young body,
Rubs it with olive oil, and settles down for a nap
In a cozy corner of the house, all on a winter's day,

While down in the godforsaken, freezing water 585
The Boneless One gnaws his own foot away,
No light filtering down to show him a feeding ground.
Sun's making his rounds over the black folks' land
And hardly shines on us Greeks at all.

590   Then horned and hornless creatures of the forest
       Go skittering up hillsides, teeth chattering
       Pitifully, all of them looking for the same thing,
       Frantic to find shelter, some cozy lair
       In the hollow rock. Like old Mr. Three Legs
595   Down the road, his back broken and head bent over,
       They skulk around trying to get out of the snow.

       Take my advice and wear protective clothing then.
       First, a soft cloak and a full-length tunic—
       You want a heavy weft woven on a thin warp—
600   Put those on so your hair won't bristle
       And you don't get goosebumps all over your body.
       Next, lace on your feet a pair of good-fitting boots,
       Felt-lined, made from the hide of a slaughtered ox.
       And make yourself a slicker out of good kidskins
605   (Stitch 'em with ox-sinew), to keep the rain off.
       Do all this as soon as it turns cold. On your head
       Wear a good felt cap, so your ears won't get wet.

       Mornings come cold when the North Wind falls in,
       And from the starry sky an early mist settles
610   Over rich men's fields (helps the wheat grow).
       The moisture gets drawn up from running rivers
       And is raised up high above earth on currents of wind.
       Sometimes it falls in the evening as rain, or it might
       Blow as a storm when clouds come in from the North.
615   Finish your work and get home before it, else
       A dark cloud is liable to pour down on you
       And soak your clothes right through to the skin.
       Keep an eye out for it.

                                    This is the hardest month,
620   Wintry, hard for sheep and hard for men.
       Put your oxen on half-rations then, but your man
       On more than half. The long nights are a help here.

       Mind all this until the year comes to an end,
       And balance off the days against the nights
625   Until Mother Earth bears her various fruits.

Spring

When Zeus has finished sixty winter days
After the solstice, then the star
Arcturus leaves Ocean's holy stream
Glittering bright, its first rising at dusk.
Soon after, Pandion's keening daughter   *630*
The swallow appears, as Spring just begins.
Best prune your vines before she comes your way.
But when the House-Toter leaves the ground
And climbs up plants (fleeing the Pleiades)
There's no more digging in vineyards then.   *635*
Time to sharpen sickles and rouse your workers.
No sitting in the shade or sleeping till dawn
During harvest season, when skin's parched by the sun.
Get a move on and bring in your crops,
Waking up early so your livelihood will be sure.   *640*

Dawn marks off a third of your workday,
Dawn gives you a good start on journey & job,
Dawn, whose light puts many men on the road
            And the yoke on many an ox.

Summer

But when the thistle's in bloom, and the cicada   *645*
Chirps from its perch on a branch, pouring down
Shrill song from its wings in the withering heat,
Then goats are plumpest, wine at its best, women
Most lustful, but men at their feeblest, since Sirius
Scorches head and knees, and skin shrivels up.   *650*
Time then for Biblian wine under a shady rock,
A milk cake from goats that are drying up,
Flesh of a wood-bred heifer that hasn't yet calved,
And of firstling kids.
                        Time to drink sparkling wine   *655*
Sitting in the shade, heart satisfied with food,
Face turned toward the cooling West Wind,
And from a spring that flows continually clear
Without any silt, time to pour out

660   Three parts water and a fourth part wine.

       When Orion's strong stars first appear,
       Order your workers to winnow Demeter's
       Holy grain, on a rolled threshing floor
       In a well-aired place. Put it up carefully in jars
665   With a scoop, and when you have all your goods
       Neatly stored in your house, go ahead and get
       Your hired hand, and look for a servant girl,
       Childless—no use having her nursing.
       And take good care of your jagged-toothed dog,
670   Don't stint him his food, or some dark night
       A Day-Sleeper will make off with all your stuff.
       Bring in fodder and litter for your oxen and mules,
       Then give your men a break and unhitch your team.

       When Sirius and Orion have come to mid-sky
675   And rose-fingered Dawn looks at Arcturus,
       Cut off your grape clusters, Perses my boy,
       Bring them to the house, expose them to the sun
       For ten days, shade them for five,
       And on the next day drain off the wine
680   Into jars, a gift from smiling Dionysos.

       When the Pleiades, Hyades and Orion go down,
       Remember now, it's the season to plow,

       And may the seed set well in the ground.

Seafaring

       If you ever get the urge for hard seafaring
685   When the Pleiades chased by gigantic Orion
       Fall into the misty sea, well forget it:
       All sorts of winds are whipping around then.
       Too late to have a boat on the wine-colored water.
       Work the earth then, remembering what I told you.

690   Haul your boat onto shore and pack stones
       All around it, to keep off the wind's damp.

And pull the bilge-plug so rain won't rot the hull.
Stow all the gear and tackle of your sea-going craft
Away in your house, tucking the sails neatly,
And hang the polished rudder up in the smoke.   *695*
Then sit tight until the sailing season comes.
When it does, haul that swift ship down to the sea
And load her up so you can bring home a good profit.

     That's what Pa used to do, Perses, you know,
     Sail on ships, trying to make ends meet,   *700*
     Till one day he came here—crossed a deal
     Of open water in a black ship—and left
     His hometown Aiolian Kyme for good.
     You can bet he wasn't running from prosperity
     But from the awful poverty Zeus gives to men.   *705*
     He settled by Helikon, in this woebegone town,
     Askra,
         bad in winter,
             godawful in summer,
                 nice never.   *710*

Anyway, Perses, remember: there's a season
For everything, but especially for sailing.
And you can praise a small ship,
But put your freight in a large one.
The bigger the cargo, the greater the profit,   *715*
If the winds hold back their blasted gales.

So if you ever turn your addled wits to trade
To rid yourself of debt and gnawing hunger,
I can teach you the rhythms of the churning sea,
Though sailing's not my line. As far as ships go,   *720*
I've never sailed in one on the open sea
Except to Euboia once from Aulis, where the Akhaians once
Waited out a stretch of bad weather, the army mustered
From all holy Hellas bound for Troy and Troy's women.

     Crossed over to Khalkis, I did, to the funeral games   *725*
     For old Amphidamas. The great man's sons had put up
     Prizes aplenty for the contests, and I'm proud to say

I won in the songfest and took home an eared tripod.
Dedicated it to the Helikonian Muses, on the very spot
730   Where they first set me on the road to clear song.

That's the sum of my experience with pegged & dowelled ships.
Still, I can teach you the mind of Zeus the Storm King,
Since the Muses have taught me ineffable song.

Fifty days after the solstice, toward the end
735   Of summer, the season of scorching heat,
Comes the sailing season. You won't wreck
Your ship then, nor the sea drown your men,
Unless Poseidon Earthshaker has a mind otherwise,
Or the Lord of Immortals *wants* to destroy them.
740   These two set the terms of good and evil alike.
But the winds are easy to judge then
And the sea's gentle. You can trust
That swift ship of yours to the breeze
Without a care, haul her down to the sea
745   And load on all your cargo.
But go as fast as you can, and hurry
Back home. Don't wait for the new wine
Or the autumn rains, or the stormy season coming on
With high winds from the South that stir up the sea
750   And make sailing grim business under a wet autumn sky.

There's another season for sailing, in the spring:
When new fig-leaves at the tip of the branch
Open up to the size of a crow's footprint,
You can get on the sea. That's the spring sailing season,
755   Not that I like it. It just doesn't sit well with me.
It's borrowed time, and you'll find it hard
To get away with. Still, men are foolish
And ignorant enough to try even *that*.
Money's life. That's the human condition.
760   But it's a terrible thing, to die in the waves.

Well, as I say, think all these things over,
And don't put all you have in the hold of a ship.
Leave the better part behind, load the lesser aboard.

It's disastrous to run into trouble at sea,
Just as it's disastrous to load a wagon too full,   *765*
Break the axle, and have the whole load ruined.
So mind your measures, and remember:

Everything you do is best done in season.

Marrying

Marry at the right age. Bring home a wife
When you're just about thirty, give or take   *770*
A few years. That's marrying in season.

A woman ought to wed when she's five years a woman.
Marry her virgin so you can teach her prudent ways.
The best girl to marry is the girl next door,
But have a good look around and make sure first   *775*
That marrying her won't make you a joke to your neighbors.

A man couldn't steal anything better than a good wife,
Just as nothing is more horrible than a bad one,
Some freeloader who roasts her man without a fire
And serves him up to a raw old age.   *780*

A List of Don'ts to Avoid the Gods' Anger

Don't make a friend equal to a brother.
But if you do, don't start any trouble,
And don't say anything you don't really mean.
But if he starts it, and says something
Or does something you don't like, remember   *785*
To pay him back double. Then if he makes up
With you and wants to set things to rights,
Take him up on it. It's a sorry man
Makes one friend then another. But you,
Make sure your face matches your mind.   *790*

Don't get yourself a name for taking in
Too many guests or none at all, nor for being
Either a friend of louts or a mocker of lords.

Don't throw a man's poverty up in his face.
795   He's already hurting, and it comes from the gods.
The best treasure in the world is a tongue
That knows when to stop, the greatest pleasure
Is when it goes as it should. Say bad things
And you're sure to hear worse yourself.

800   Don't be tiresome at a potluck dinner:
It's good entertainment and cheap at that.

Don't pour a libation of wine at dawn
To Zeus or any other immortal god
Without first washing your hands:
805   They'll spit your prayers out.

Don't piss standing up while facing the sun.
Between sunset and sunrise, remember,
Don't piss on the road or on the roadside,
Or naked. The blessed gods own the night.
810   A religious man sits down, if he's got any sense,
Or he goes by the wall of an enclosed courtyard.

Don't let your privates be seen smeared with semen
Near the hearth at home. Be careful to avoid this.

Don't beget children after coming home
815   From a burial. Wait until after a feast of the gods.

Don't ever set foot in a river you're fording
Without saying your prayers first. Gaze deep
Into the current as you wash your hands
In the precious white water. Whoever crosses
820   A river unwashed (I mean hands *and* wickedness)
The gods visit with nemesis and suffering later.

Don't trim the dry from the five-branched quick
Using honed, flashing steel at a feast of the gods.

Don't ever put a jug on top of the mixing bowl
825   When folks are drinking. It's deadly bad luck.

Don't leave the wood rough on a house you're building,
Or a chattering crow might perch on it and croak.

Don't eat from impure pots, nor wash from them
Either. There's a terrible vengeance in them.

Don't let a boy of twelve sit on gravestones and such. 830
It's a bad thing to do. Makes a man unmanly.
Nor a twelve month old, it comes to the same thing.

Don't wash in a woman's bath-water,
Which for a time has a bitter vengeance in it.

Don't, if you come across a sacrifice burning, 835
Find fault with what the fire consumes.
The god will visit you with nemesis for sure.

Don't piss in the mouth of a river that flows to the sea,
Nor in springs either. And don't ever shit in them.

That's the way to behave. And try to avoid being 840
The object of talk. A bad reputation is easy to get,
Difficult to endure, and hard to get rid of.
Talk never really dies, not when so many folks
Are busy with her. Talk too is some kind of a god.

Days

Days come from Zeus. Keep good track of them, 845
And inform your workers that among civil folk
Who reckon things rightly, the Thirtieth is the day
For scheduling work and distributing supplies.

Here are the days as they come from Zeus in his wisdom:

The First, Fourth and Seventh 850
    On which Leto bore
    Gold-bladed Apollo
    Are all holy days.

The Eighth and Ninth
855   Are two days at least
                 Of the waxing month
                 Good for labor.

The Eleventh and Twelfth
                 Are excellent days
860   Both for shearing sheep
                 And bringing in sheaves.
But the Twelfth is much better than the Eleventh,
For on that day the wispy spider spins her web
In broad daylight, and the Provident One scrapes up her pile.
865   A woman should set up her loom and get along in her work.

The Thirteenth of the waxing month
                 Is a bad day to start seeding
                 But the best for transplanting.

The Sixth of the midmonth
870   Is very unfavorable for plants
                 But good for a male to be born,
                 Though not favorable for a girl
                 Either to be born or get married.

Nor is the first Sixth good for a girl to be born,
875   Though it's a fair day for gelding kids and sheep
Or for throwing up a fence around your sheepfold.
It's a good day for male births, but a boy born then
Likely will quarrel and lie, cheat, plot and scheme.

On the Eighth of the month
880   Geld your boars
                 And bellowing bulls.
But geld stubborn mules on the Twelfth.

On the great Twentieth
                 In broad daylight
885   Give birth to a sage
                 With a luminous mind.

The Tenth is excellent
> For a boy to be born,

But the middle Fourth
> Is good for a girl.   *890*
> Now tame to your hand
> Shambling cattle & sheep,
> Fanged dog & stubborn mule.
But try to stay clear of trouble and heartache
On the Fourth of the waxing and waning month: *895*
Both of these days are doomed and fatal.
Do bring your bride home on the Fourth,
But look for omens that suit this business.

Run for cover on Fifths, awful days, dreadful days.
They say that on a Fifth the Furies assisted   *900*
At the birth of Oath, born of Eris to torment the forsworn.

On the middle Seventh
> Look sharp, throw Demeter's grain
> Onto a well-rolled threshing-floor.
> Woodcutters now hew timber   *905*
> For houses, beams for ships.

On the Fourth start work on the ship's slender hull.

The middle Ninth gets better towards evening.
The first Ninth is entirely harmless for men,
A good day to plant, a good day to be born   *910*
For man or woman, a day never altogether bad.

Few people know that the third Ninth is the best day
> For opening a wine jar,
> Putting a yoke on oxen
> On horses and mules,   *915*
> For hauling a trim launch
> Down to the wine-colored sea.
Few people call this day by its right name.

Open a jar on the Fourth. The holiest day of all
920   Is the middle Fourth. The Twenty-fourth is very good
When it's dawning, but gets worse towards evening.

These days are valuable for men upon earth,
But the rest are variable, fateless, don't mean a thing.
Everybody praises different days, but few folks know them.
925   Sometimes a day's a stepmother, sometimes a mother.
As far as days go, you're doing well if you know all this,
And get your work done without offending the gods,
If you read your birds right and manage not to transgress.

FINIS

title: In the surviving literature, *Works and Days* as a title for this composite work does not appear before the second century CE and refers, properly speaking, to only two sections of it (427–683 [381–617] and 845–928 [765–828]). It no doubt went by this title (sometimes shortened to *Works*), at least from the Hellenistic period.

1–21 [1–10] The prologue or proem takes the form of a short hymn to Zeus, introduced by an invitation to the Muses (cf. *Theogony* 1 [1], 35 [34]).

19 [10] *Perses:* Hesiod's brother is a mute persona, a silent audience integrated into the presumably fictional frame of the wisdom poetry. An analogy can be found in the mute persona of Kyrnus in the poetry attributed to Theognis.

21 [11] *Strife:* This may be read as a correction or revision of both the Hesiodic and the Homeric genealogies of Strife, last of the children of Night in the *Theogony* (213–27 [211–25]). That primal Strife, it seems, might better be called "competition" and the more familiar, destructive Strife (presumably the monstrous and "insatiably raving" Strife, "sister and companion of man-killing Ares" of *Iliad* 4.440–41) is here said to be a younger deity, of unspecified genealogy.

44 [29] *market:* The distractions of the disputes and lawsuits of the *agora* are among the stock motifs of Attic comedy that have their background in Hesiodic poetry, but their relevance to Athenian life of the fifth century is far easier to imagine than their role in rural Askra, the imagined setting for Hesiod's advice to Perses. Lawsuits belong to the negative Strife, as gainful competition is the province of the positive one.

51 [35] *feud:* A lawsuit over their inheritance is the primary motivation both for Hesiod's advice to his brother and for the evocation of the two Strifes.

55 [38–39] The "bribe-eating lords" (*basileis,* "kings") give us the first glimpse of the structure of Hesiodic society, characteristically viewed from the perspective of the weak and exploited.

57 [41] *mallows and asphodel:* Plants characteristic of impoverished soil, and perhaps to be taken here as the food of the very poor—gatherers rather than farmers.

58–59 [42] That the spiteful gods hide the livelihood that might otherwise come easily to mankind is fundamental to the Hesiodic account of things.

66 [48] With the Prometheus story as told here (65–125 [45–99]), compare *Theogony* 536–618 [535–616], where the withholding of fire by the gods is explained as retaliation for the trick by which Prometheus established the practice of sacrifice to the advantage of mankind.

89 [70] *Gimpy:* elsewhere "Lame God," lit. "lame-in-both-legs," a standard, Homeric epithet of Hephaistos, the lame smith god.

91 [72] *Owl-Eyed Goddess:* Athene's frequent epithet *glaukopis* has been interpreted in various ways since antiquity. It may refer to the color of her eyes ("grey-eyed") or to their size and appearance, or there may be lurking here a reference to a partially theriomorphic manifestation of the goddess (unattested iconographically) that was "owl-faced." In Homer, Hera is similarly called *boopis:* "ox-eyed" or "ox-faced."

101 [81] *Pandora:* The line explains the etymology of the name (*pandora* or "all-gift"). The name itself is ambiguous, however, and capable of having either one of two senses: "giver-of-all" or "receiver-of-all" i.e. "endowed by all" (the sense here). It is possible that the former is more natural and that the etymology here ironically undercuts what would otherwise be taken as a laudatory epithet.

104 [84] *Epimetheus:* Prometheus and his brother have transparent names as well: "foresight" and "hindsight." But just what is their relationship to mankind? The story as told here (and in the *Theogony*) makes Epimetheus sound very much like a mortal. Otherwise, why would his acceptance of the woman bring all those ills down on mankind's head? Clearly, she is introduced into the world of men and brings all those "gifts" with her.

115 [94] *big jar:* What we know traditionally as "Pandora's box" is in this oldest version of the story actually a large storage jar, or *pithos*. The largest of these, stored beneath the floor with the mouth emerging, might have a capacity of hundreds of gallons.

117 [96] *Hope:* There is clearly a lapse of logic here. What was Hope doing in there with the evil things that afflict mankind? It seems clear that Hope was left for mankind as a consolation, a desirable possession after the release of the bad things, but in that case Hope's companions, the escaped contents of the jar, should have positive associations. Perhaps an earlier version is implied, in which the opening of the storage jar had the opposite effect, releasing *good* things that subsequently eluded mankind.

126 [106] *If you want. . . .:* Transitions of this sort within the poem seem to underline the freedom of the poet's choice, as the performance develops, among the traditional material at his disposal.

126 [106] ff. The myth of the five ages of mankind (Golden, Silver, Bronze, Heroes, and Iron) in its Hesiodic form is lacking in symmetry and seems to represent the adaptation of several preexisting anthropologies. It appears to be linear, but Hesiod's wish that he'd lived before *or after* the Iron Age (203 [175]) may imply a latent cyclical conception of history. What is certain is that this world view as it develops here is unrelentingly pessimistic, and mankind is said to have been created at a stage as near perfection as possible, and then to have evolved ever downwards to the radically depleted world of present experience, on the verge of moral chaos in the form of total alienation from the principles of shame and justice. The myth functions as a second, alternative (and not entirely compatible) explanation of just *why* we (and especially Perses) find ourselves in the fix we are in, so that we need Hesiod's advice to see us through.

129–47 [109–26] The Golden Age in the time of Kronos saw newly created mankind free of two major ills: old age and want. After their painless existence in this sustaining world and a sleep-like death, they became divine avengers and benefactors, representing the principle of justice. Thus they must be the thirty thousand guardian "spirits" mentioned below (292 [252]). These ancient "races of men" populate the spiritual realms of the present in Hesiod's imagination.

148–64 [126–42] The Silver Age seems to owe its inferiority primarily to the prolongation of infancy, first literally, then in the form of infantile violence as adults. This "lack of wits" disrupts relations among men and between men and gods and they, unlike their predecessors, disappear because they provoke divine anger. Their current status as "blessed underground mortals" points to some sort of ancestor or "Hero" cult, but it is difficult to be more specific as to its nature.

165–77 [143–55] The Bronze Age amplifies the violence on the human plane, though here the gods are not mentioned, and the violent mortals put an end to each other with no help beyond that of Death. Their life cycles seem to have been less odd than those of their predecessors, but they themselves were physically monstrous, "shapeless hulks" expressing their violent natures in the flesh. Their bronze trappings, owed no doubt to the emphasis on bronze in the tradition of military epic represented by the *Iliad*, represent a redefinition of the sequence of races. Whereas gold and silver are purely symbolic, representing a hierarchy of value, the Bronze Age gets its name from its technology. These warriors die nameless, and this seems to be the principal difference between them and the subsequent race.

178–97 [156–73c] The race of Heroes is aberrant in two ways: 1) it is not named after a metal, and 2) it is better than its predecessor. If the Bronze Age was a time of unalloyed violence, it must be somehow reconciled with Homeric epic and the poetic traditions of exemplary heroic warfare. Hence the insertion of this "age," Hesiod's way of saying that in that age of violence there were also the heroic wars of epic. But this time, there are names, and memory (preserved in song): Oidipous and Helen, Thebes and Troy. These Heroes are now oddly isolated from the present world, where those first two races still have their role, on the remote "Isles of the Blessed"—a fate similar to the one that Homer's Proteus promised to Menelaus (*Od.* 4.561–570).

195–200 [173a–e] The bracketed lines do not occur in the text of the poem as the medieval manuscripts preserve it, but two papyri and remarks of ancient commentators make it clear that they occurred at this point at some stage in the poem's history. The Isles of the Blessed thus recapitulate the Golden Age, likewise ruled over by Kronos (here released from his bondage with the other Titans in Tartaros (732–34 [729–31], 820–21 [813–14]).

198–234 [173d–201] The Iron Age, Hesiod's and our own, is less succinctly defined and delineated, since it continues and is the framework of the rest of the poem. In fact, much of this passage is in the future tense, and takes the form of a prophecy of escalating violence and neglect of justice, traditional values, oaths, etc. Though destruction by Zeus hangs over us, the climax of the description is the withdrawal of Shame and Nemesis, ominously leaving us to our own devices.

235–45 [202–12] This beast "fable," probably the earliest recorded in European literature, shifts the thread of the poem from our descent into our current dilemma to the general issue of the justice that our age has lost. Like all fables, it calls out for interpretation, for a "moral tag" to explain it, but Hesiod makes Perses (and us) listen to a considerable harangue on justice, criminality, and retribution, before supplying that tag at 316–22 [274–80]. What the hawk articulates here is an account of the world appropriate to hawks (and nightingales, fish, and so forth): In the absence of justice, the natural world is founded on force, and the strong devour the weak if they choose. What the fable does not tell us (because hawks and nightingales don't know such things) is that the realm of human experience is different, and the difference is justice.

275 [236–37] *Never travel on ships:* While the poem offers considerable advice on merchant seafaring (684 [618] ff.), that information is decidedly

at odds with its general value system, which is bound to the land, so it is no surprise that the people of the city ruled by justice, whom the earth sustains, have no desire to go to sea.

276–85 [238–47] There are some striking asymmetries in the portraits of the city ruled by justice and its opposite. Everyone must observe justice to win divine favor and prosperity for the community. That the criminality and "violence" (Gk. *hubris*) (276 [238]) of one individual can bring down retribution on a whole city suggests the case of Paris and Troy.

286 [248] *Rulers and Lords* (Gk. *basileis*): See on 55, above. Hesiod is characteristically critical of those in power, and claims the right both to insult them and to lecture them. They are "bribe-eating" lords again at 303 [264].

287–95 [249–57] See on 129–47, above.

316–22 [274–80] See on 235–45, above.

336 [293] ff. Up to this point, Hesiod has explained to Perses in two different ways just why this diminished world refuses to sustain us unless we are willing to work for a living. The second of these accounts, the ages of man, has led into a lengthy praise of justice and condemnation of criminality. The progressive alienation of mankind from justice has provided an adequate background for this, and Perses' unfair abrogation of more than his fair share of the paternal property is part and parcel of mankind's general rottenness (360–61 [315–16], though in fact this dispute seems to fade from memory as the poem progresses). The unspoken assumption seems to be that Perses might be expected, in the face of need, to resort to criminality rather than work, and so this option has to be considered before proceeding. From this point on, though, until the beginning of the *Days* (845 [765]), the focus on the exhortation to labor, extended by practical advice on how to maximize the results of that labor and protect its fruits, forms the clear thread of the poem, closely interwoven at first with the theme of justice.

336–40 [293–97] This hierarchy naturally secures the place of the didactic poet—of Hesiod himself—in the larger world. He is the preeminent giver of "advice" and so serves the "good man" (Gk. *esthlos*), who acknowledges the shortcomings of his own wisdom.

347–49 [304–6] With this line compare *Theogony* 598–603, where in a more elaborate simile, women are compared to drones in the hive.

355 [311] From here on until the beginning of the account of the agricultural year (430 [383]), the poetic language tends more and more toward

the gnomic or proverbial, and the connection between one bit of advice and the next is often strained. Compare 781 [707] ff. Perses is warned of the hunger and shame of poverty and the retribution awaiting the criminal, advised on how to stay on the right side of the gods through sacrifice, and of his neighbors by judicious entertainment and gift-giving.

402 [356] "Give" [Gk. *Dos*] and "Gimmee" [Gk. *Harpaks*] provide nice examples of the ease and wit with which this traditional, gnomic language invents personifications or, more accurately, gives personal form to abstractions.

422 [376] The injunction to have only a single son is interesting in the context of Hesiod's general advice on family planning. The threat that hangs over the bachelor is explicit in the *Theogony* (605–9 [603–7]): He'll lack support in his old age, and his property will be dispersed by distant relatives. This is the only reason to tolerate the miseries of marriage. Multiple sons would pose a parallel threat to the household and its property—the example of Hesiod and Perses inevitably comes to mind. Given this danger, it is striking that Hesiod uncharacteristically hedges here and gives conflicting advice: One son is best, but a larger family is all right, too.

430 [383] *The Pleiades:* A small but striking cluster of (to most eyes) six stars of nearly equal brightness lying in the constellation Taurus. They are here said to be "Born of Atlas," and a fragment that may come from the *Catalogue of Women* gives them names (seven of them, and this is the traditional number). Along with Sirius, Orion, and Arcturus, they mark by their rising and setting the principal events of Hesiod's agricultural year. Their disappearance from the late fall sky, after the rains have softened the ground, is a signal to plow; their reappearance in the morning sky in May, a signal to harvest.

445–46 [395–96] Now we learn, rather belatedly, that the occasion of this lecture is that Perses is in bad shape and has come to ask his brother for a handout. This claim is neither anticipated nor repeated, but it goes a long way to explain just why Perses has to keep quiet and listen while his brother lectures him and insults him.

469 [417] Sirius, the bright star near the constellation Orion, known already to Homer (*Iliad* 22.29) as "Orion's Dog," becomes visible for Hesiod in the night sky just before sunrise in July, the hottest part of the year, after remaining invisible for months. In September, when it is overhead more and more at night, the heat breaks and the fall rains come. This is the time when Hesiod advises cutting wood. It's at this point as

well that he describes the construction of wagon and plow, but this is surely only a narrative convenience, leading into the description of the next seasonal activity, the late fall plowing.

501 [448] Hesiod recommends taking the sound of the migrating cranes overhead as a signal to plow and to sow grain, so this event must coincide with the setting of the Pleiades (432–33 [384], above), by West's calculation, about the beginning of November. The poet concedes, though, that some plow as late as late December (perhaps by preference, though the implication seems to be that it is from laziness or lack of preparedness) and that the success or failure of this strategy depends on spring rains.

522 [465] *Zeus-in-the-ground* (Gk. *Zeus khthonios*): Zeus as protector of crops.

558 [497] *a thick foot:* Swollen feet were a proverbial consequence of famine.

565 [504] *Lenaion:* The only month mentioned by name in the Hesiodic corpus was not in Boeotian calendars. It was an Ionian month, and though it was not in the Attic calendar, the Athenians did have an important winter festival called the Lenaia. This is one of the most striking illustrations of the fact that while the Hesiodic poems advertise their connection to the Valley of the Muses in western Boeotia, the content of the poetry is Panhellenic and has little about it that is specifically Boeotian.

586 [524] *Boneless One:* Apparently a kenning (fixed poetic metaphor) or perhaps a colloquial expression for "octopus." Their penchant for self-mutilation was widely noted in antiquity.

594 [533] *Mr. Three Legs:* As in the riddle of the Sphinx, a kenning for a person who walks with a cane.

628 [566] *Arcturus:* The first appearance of this bright star (in the constellation Boötes) in the evening sky after sunset occurs, according to Hesiod, about February 20 (sixty days after the solstice), and tells the farmer to prune his vines.

630 [568] *Pandion's keening daughter:* Philomela, daughter of a legendary king of Athens named Pandion, was raped by her brother-in-law, Tereus. After cooking Tereus' son and serving him to his father for dinner, she and her sister Procne escaped, and as he was about to catch them, all three were turned into birds. Philomela, who was turned into a swallow, thus comes to stand for all swallows.

633 [571] *House-Toter:* A kenning for "snail." It is not clear why Hesiod should claim that snails climb up plants especially in May, when the

Pleiades have risen and the harvest is near. Note also that he has leapt about three months since the vine-pruning in February. The wheat, planted after the rains the previous fall, has matured through the winter and spring, and in May the grass dries up, and the grain ripens for harvest in late May and June.

645 [582] The shrill drone of the cicadas is the most characteristic sound of the Mediterranean landscape in the heat of summer.

649 [587] See on 469, above. In the "Dog Days," Sirius becomes visible just before sunrise and so was thought to be in the sky with the sun all day, causing the intense heat.

651 [589] *Biblian wine:* Apparently, wine from a special grape first cultivated in a Thracian locality called Biblos, but the actual reference is in doubt.

660 [596] The Greeks seem always to have watered their wine (and drinking it straight might be an occasion of reproach aimed at Macedonians and other hard-drinking "barbarians")—but this mixture is extreme. Clearly the emphasis is on the desired effect of the cool spring water.

671 [605] *Day-sleeper:* Clearly a kenning for the thief who works by night.

674 [609] Another three-month leap, from the threshing which must follow closely on the May-June harvest, to the grape harvest in September, about a month and a half before the cycle begins again with the plowing and sowing after the arrival of the autumn rains.

684–768 [618–94] Hesiod's advice on seafaring is difficult to reconcile with the fictional dramatic situation of Hesiod lecturing his brother in Askra, some distance from salt water, and it is here that we get more autobiographical detail of surprising specificity. Hesiod tells us that the brothers' father came by ship from Kyme, southernmost of the Aiolian cities in Asia Minor, and that Hesiod himself at some time in the past went off by ship to Khalkis in Euboea to compete in the funeral games of a king named Amphidamas.

685 [619] Hesiod begins by telling Perses when *not* to sail—that is, at plowing time (but not on the basis that he would miss his plowing, but for the more compelling reason that that is not a time of predictable winds).

699–710 [633–40] This autobiographical passage, with its unflattering portrait of Hesiod's hometown, complements the prologue of the *Theogony* and constitutes the core of the Hesiodic self-portrait. On Askra, see the Introduction, pp. 2–4.

720 [649] *not my line:* Hesiod insists that he's never been taught sailing, never developed the skill, at the same time he advertises his ability to teach it. This assertion is more paradoxical than it might appear on the surface and should be compared to the gnomic advice in 254 [218]: "fools learn . . . the hard way." Hesiod's knowledge is from another source—the Muses (731–33 [660–62])—and his poetry reminds us often that this is the better path to knowledge.

720–30 [650–59]) Ever since Plutarch, readers of Hesiod have had doubts about the authenticity of this account of Hesiod's only sea voyage. It is very likely that it was interpolated into the poem in order to provide a pedigree for an actual tripod displayed in the precinct of the Muses on Helikon.

734 [663] The Greek is not entirely clear on the period designated (and the ambiguity is preserved here). Did sailing season *start* fifty days after the solstice (i.e. August 10 until, say, early October, to get home before the rains) or did it *last* for fifty days, solstice (June 21) to about August 10? The latter is more likely to be Hesiod's point and is the easier way to construe the Greek, but there were differences of opinion in the matter even in antiquity. In summer, the winds in the eastern Mediterranean may be strong, but they are at least consistent, blowing from the north.

751–60 [678–88] The spring sailing season would be in late April and May—just before the grain harvest.

769–80 [695–705] The misogyny of the poem down to this point is, if anything, somewhat mitigated in the advice on marriage. It is generally characteristic of the poem to put everything in a bad light, to focus on the dangers and threats inherent in all the aspects of life it gives advice on, and clearly women are viewed as a necessary evil and marriage a reluctant concession to the need to produce an heir. The observation that "a man couldn't steal anything better than a good wife" nevertheless goes some way toward restoring balance.

781–844 [706–64] This motley collection of gnomic lore has two foci: socialization and ritual purity. Reputation is clearly the key element in social relations, evoked early in the series (791 [715]) and at the end (840–44 [760–64]). The rest of the advice has to do with avoiding various sorts of defilement offensive to the gods.

845 [765] ff. The final section of the poem is the *Days*, properly so called. It is an elaborate excursus on the sort of superstitious lore that survives

in vestigial form in American society in the form of wariness of Friday the 13th. It is separated from the preceding performance of proverbial lore by a line (845 [765]) that echoes the line that served as introduction to the proverbs ([706] represented here by the title between 780 and 781), and clearly marks the "days" as a new category of useful information whose observance will provide benefit to the listener. The system of numbering is somewhat odd from our perspective, and does not seem to correspond exactly to that of any known Greek community, though in its broad outlines it conforms to patterns found in Athens and other cities. Most dates will be comprehensible if the reader bears in mind that the roughly 30 days of the lunar month are here thought of as three "tens." Thus the "middle fourth" is the fourteenth. In Athens, the third "ten" (the waning moon) was counted backwards, but it is impossible to know whether Hesiod's "fourth of the . . . waning month" is the 24th (counting forward) or the 27th (counting backwards).

864 [778] *Provident One:* "knower" (Gk. *idris*): A kenning for "ant."

THEOGONY

Invocation to the Muses

Begin our singing with the Helikonian Muses,
Who possess Mount Helikon, high and holy,
And near its violet-stained spring on petalsoft feet
Dance circling the altar of almighty Kronion,

And having bathed their silken skin in Permessos   5
Or in Horse Spring or the sacred creek Olmeios,
They begin their choral dance on Helikon's summit
So lovely it pangs, and with power in their steps
Ascend veiled and misted in palpable air
Treading the night, and in a voice beyond beauty   10
They chant:

   Zeus Aegisholder and his lady Hera
   Of Argos, in gold sandals striding,
   And the Aegisholder's girl, owl-eyed Athene,
   And Phoibos Apollo and arrowy Artemis,   15
   Poseidon earth-holder, earthquaking god,
   Modest Themis and Aphrodite, eyelashes curling,
   And Hebe goldcrowned and lovely Dione,
   Leto and Iapetos and Kronos, his mind bent,
   Eos and Helios and glowing Selene,   20
   Gaia, Okeanos, and the black one, Night,

And the whole eerie brood of the eternal Immortals.

And they once taught Hesiod the art of singing verse,
While he pastured his lambs on holy Helikon's slopes.
And this was the very first thing they told me,   25
The Olympian Muses, daughters of Zeus Aegisholder:

"Hillbillies and bellies, poor excuses for shepherds:
We know how to tell many believable lies,
But also, when we want to, how to speak the plain truth."

30   So spoke the daughters of great Zeus, mincing their words.
      And they gave me a staff, a branch of good sappy laurel,
      Plucking it off, spectacular. And they breathed into me
      A voice divine, so I might celebrate past and future.
      And they told me to hymn the generation of the eternal gods,
35   But always to sing of themselves, the Muses, first and last.

      But why all this about oak tree or stone?

      Start from the Muses: when they sing for Zeus Father
      They thrill the great mind deep in Olympos,
      Telling what is, what will be, and what has been,
40   Blending their voices, and weariless the sound
      Flows sweet from their lips and spreads like lilies,
      And Zeus' thundering halls shine with laughter,
      And Olympos' snowy peaks and the halls of the gods
      Echo the strains as their immortal chanting
45   Honors first the primordial generation of gods
      Whom in the beginning Earth and Sky bore,
      And the divine benefactors born from them;
      And, second, Zeus, the Father of gods and men,
      Mightiest of the gods and strongest by far;
50   And then the race of humans and of powerful Giants.
      And Zeus' mind in Olympos is thrilled by the song
      Of the Olympian Muses, the Storm King's daughters.

      They were born on Pieria after our Father Kronion
      Mingled with Memory, who rules Eleutherae's hills.
55   She bore them to be a forgetting of troubles,
      A pause in sorrow. For nine nights wise Zeus
      Mingled with her in love, ascending her sacred bed
      In isolation from the other Immortals.
      But when the time drew near, and the seasons turned,
60   And the moons had waned, and the many days were done,
      She bore nine daughters, all of one mind, with song
      In their breasts, with hearts that never failed,
      Near the topmost peak of snowcapped Olympos.

      There are their polished dancing grounds, their fine halls,
65   And the Graces and Desire have their houses close by,

And all is in bloom. And they move in the dance, intoning
The careful ways of the gods, celebrating the customs
Of all the Immortals in a voice enchanting and sweet.
Then they process to Olympos, a glory of pure
Sound and dance, and the black earth shrieks with delight   70
As they sing, and the drum of their footfalls rises like love
As they go to their father. He is king in the sky,
He holds the vajra thunder and flashing lightning.
He defeated his father Kronos by force, and He ordained
Laws for the gods and assigned them their rights.   75

Thus sing the Muses who have their homes on Olympos,

   The nine daughters born of great Zeus,

    Klio, Euterpe, Thalia, Melpomene,
    Terpsichore, Erato, Polyhymnia, Ourania,

   And Kalliope, the most important of all,   80

For she keeps the company of reverend kings.
When the daughters of great Zeus will honor a lord
Whose lineage is divine, and look upon his birth,
They distill a sweet dew upon his tongue,
And from his mouth words flow like honey. The people   85
All look to him as he arbitrates settlements
With judgments straight. He speaks out in sure tones
And soon puts an end even to bitter disputes.
A sound-minded ruler, when someone is wronged,
Sets things to rights in the public assembly,   90
Conciliating both sides with ease.
He comes to the meeting place propitiated as a god,
Treated with respect, preeminent in the crowd.
Such is the Muses' sacred gift to men.
For though it is singers and lyre players   95
That come from the Muses and far-shooting Apollo
And kings come from Zeus, happy is the man
Whom the Muses love. Sweet flows the voice from his mouth.
For if anyone is grieved, if his heart is sore
With fresh sorrow, if he is troubled, and a singer   100

Who serves the Muses chants the deeds of past men
Or the blessed gods who have their homes on Olympos,
He soon forgets his heartache, and of all his cares
He remembers none: the goddesses' gifts turn them aside.

105   Farewell Zeus's daughters, and bestow song that beguiles.
Make known the eerie brood of the eternal Immortals
Who were born of Earth and starry Sky,
And of dusky Night, and whom the salt Sea bore.
Tell how first the gods and earth came into being
110   And the rivers and the sea, endless and surging,
And the stars shining and the wide sky above;
How they divided wealth and allotted honors,
And first possessed deep-ridged Olympos.

Tell me these things, Olympian Muses,
115   From the beginning, and tell which of them came first.

The First Gods

In the beginning there was only Chaos, the Abyss,
But then Gaia, the Earth, came into being,
Her broad bosom the ever-firm foundation of all,
And Tartaros, dim in the underground depths,
120   And Eros, loveliest of all the Immortals, who
Makes their bodies (and men's bodies) go limp,
Mastering their minds and subduing their wills.

From the Abyss were born Erebos and dark Night.
And Night, pregnant after sweet intercourse
125   With Erebos, gave birth to Aether and Day.

Earth's first child was Ouranos, starry Heaven,
Just her size, a perfect fit on all sides.
And a firm foundation for the blessed gods.
And she bore the Mountains in long ranges, haunted
130   By the Nymphs who live in the deep mountain dells.
Then she gave birth to the barren, raging Sea
Without any sexual love. But later she slept with
Ouranos and bore Ocean with its deep currents,

And also: Koios, Krios, Hyperion, Iapetos,
           Theia, Rheia, Themis, Mnemosyne,   *135*
           Gold-crowned Phoibe and lovely Tethys.

The Castration of Ouranos

After them she bore a most terrible child,
Kronos, her youngest, an arch-deceiver,
And this boy hated his lecherous father.

She bore the Cyclopes too, with hearts of stone,   *140*
Brontes, Steropes and ponderous Arges,
Who gave Zeus thunder and made the thunderbolt.
In every other respect they were just like gods,
But a lone eye lay in their foreheads' middle.
They were nicknamed Cyclopes because they had   *145*
A single goggle eye in their foreheads' middle.
Strong as the dickens, and they knew their craft.

And three other sons were born to Gaia and Ouranos,
Strong, hulking creatures that beggar description,
Kottos, Briareos, and Gyges, outrageous children.   *150*
A hundred hands stuck out of their shoulders,
Grotesque, and fifty heads grew on each stumpy neck.
These monsters exuded irresistible strength.
They were Gaia's most dreaded offspring,
And from the start their father feared and loathed them.   *155*
Ouranos used to stuff all of his children
Back into a hollow of Earth soon as they were born,
Keeping them from the light, an awful thing to do,
But Heaven did it, and was very pleased with himself.

Vast Earth groaned under the pressure inside,   *160*
And then she came up with a plan, a really wicked trick.
She created a new mineral, grey flint, and formed
A huge sickle from it and showed it to her dear boys.
And she rallied them with this bitter speech:

"Listen to me, children, and we might yet get even   *165*
With your criminal father for what he has done to us.

After all, he started this whole ugly business."

They were tongue-tied with fear when they heard this.
But Kronos, whose mind worked in strange ways,
170   Got his pluck up and found the words to answer her:

"I think I might be able to bring it off, Mother.
I can't stand Father; he doesn't even deserve the name.
And after all, he started this whole ugly business."

This response warmed the heart of vast Earth.
175   She hid young Kronos in an ambush and placed in his hands
The jagged sickle. Then she went over the whole plan with him.
And now on came great Ouranos, bringing Night with him.
And, longing for love, he settled himself all over Earth.
From his dark hiding-place, the son reached out
180   With his left hand, while with his right he swung
The fiendishly long and jagged sickle, pruning the genitals
Of his own father with one swoop and tossing them
Behind him, where they fell to no small effect.
Earth soaked up all the bloody drops that spurted out,
185   And as the seasons went by she gave birth to the Furies
And to great Giants gleaming in full armor, spears in hand,
And to the Meliai, as ash-tree nymphs are generally called.

The Birth of Aphrodite

The genitalia themselves, freshly cut with flint, were thrown
Clear of the mainland into the restless, white-capped sea,
190   Where they floated a long time. A white foam from the god-flesh
Collected around them, and in that foam a maiden developed
And grew. Her first approach to land was near holy Kythera,
And from there she floated on to the island of Kypros.
There she came ashore, an awesome, beautiful divinity.
195   Tender grass sprouted up under her slender feet.
                                                    Aphrodite
Is her name in speech human and divine, since it was in foam
She was nourished. But she is also called Kythereia since
She reached Kythera, and Kyprogenes because she was born
On the surf-line of Kypros, and Philommedes because she loves

The organs of sex, from which she made her epiphany.   *200*
Eros became her companion, and ravishing Desire waited on her
At her birth and when she made her debut among the Immortals.
From that moment on, among both gods and humans,
She has fulfilled the honored function that includes
Virginal sweet-talk, lovers' smiles and deceits   *205*
And all of the gentle pleasures of sex.

But great Ouranos used to call the sons he begot
Titans, a reproachful nickname, because he thought
They had over-reached themselves and done a monstrous deed
For which vengeance later would surely be exacted.   *210*

Other Early Gods

And Night bore hateful Doom and black Fate
And Death, and Sleep and the brood of Dreams.
And sleeping with no one, the ebony goddess Night
Gave birth to Blame and agonizing Grief,
And to the Hesperides who guard the golden apples   *215*
And the fruit-bearing trees beyond glorious Ocean.
And she generated the Destinies and the merciless,
Avenging Fates, Clotho, Lachesis, and Atropos,
Who give mortals at birth good and evil to have,
And prosecute transgressions of mortals and gods.   *220*
These goddesses never let up their dread anger
Until the sinner has paid a severe penalty.
And deadly Night bore Nemesis too, more misery
For mortals; and after her, Deception and Friendship
And ruinous Old Age, and hard-hearted Eris.   *225*
And hateful Eris bore agonizing Toil,
Forgetfulness, Famine, and tearful Pains,
Battles and Fights, Murders and Manslaughters,
Quarrels, Lying Words and Words Disputatious,
Lawlessness and Recklessness, who share one nature,   *230*
And Oath, who most troubles men upon Earth
When anyone willfully swears a false oath.

And Pontos, the Sea, begot his eldest, Nereus,
True and no liar. And they call him Old Man
Because he is unerring and mild, remembers   *235*

What is right, and his mind is gentle and just.
Then Sea mated with Earth and begat great Thaumas,
And arrogant Phorkys, Keto, her cheeks lovely,
And Eurybia, a stubborn heart in her breast.

240   To Nereus and Doris, her rich hair flowing,
       Daughter of the perfect river, Ocean,
       Children were born in the barren sea,
       Divinely beautiful:

       Ploto, Eukrante, Amphitrite, and Sao,
245   Eudora, Thetis, Galene, and Glauke,
       Kymothoe, Speio, lovely Halie, and Thoe,
       Pasithea, Erato, and rose-armed Eunike,
       Melite gracious, Eulimene, Agaue,
       Doto, Proto, Dynamene, Pherousa,
250   Nesaia, Aktaia, and Protomedeia,
       Doris, Panope, and fair Galateia,
       Hippothoe lovely and rose-armed Hipponoe,
       Kymodoke who with Kymatolege
       And Amphitrite (fine sculpted ankles)
255   Calms winds and waves on the misty sea—
       Kymo, Eione, and Alimede in wreaths,
       Laughing Glaukonome and Pontoporeia,
       Leagora, Euagora, and Laomedeia,
       Poulynoe, Autonoe, and Lysianassa,
260   Lovely Euarne, features perfectly formed,
       Psamathe, graceful, and shining Menippe,
       Neso, Eupompe, Themisto, Pronoe,
       And Nemertes, who has her father's mind:

       Fifty girls born to faultless Nereus,
265   And faultless all of their skills and crafts.

       And Thaumas married deep-flowing Ocean's
       Daughter, Elektra, who bore swift Iris and
       The rich-haired Harpies, Aello and Okypetes,
       Who keep pace with stormwinds and birds
270   Flying their missions on wings swift as time.

And Keto bore to Phorkys the fair-cheeked Graiai,
Grey from their birth. Both the immortal gods
And men who go on the ground call them Graiai—
Pemphredo in robes and saffron-robed Enyo—
And the Gorgons, who live beyond glorious Ocean   275
On Night's frontier near the shrill Hesperides,
Stheno, Euryale, and Medousa, who suffered,
Being mortal, while her two sisters were deathless
And ageless too. The Dark-maned One bedded her
In a meadow soft with springtime flowers.   280
When Perseus cut the head from her neck,
Great Chrysaor leaped out, and Pegasos the horse,
So-called from the springs of Ocean nearby.
Chrysaor is named from the gold sword he holds.
Pegasos left earth, the mother of flocks, and flew   285
Off to the gods, and there he lives, in the house
Of wise Zeus, and brings him thunder and lightning.

And Chrysaor begot Geryon, with a triple head,
After mingling with Kallirhoe, Ocean's daughter.
Mighty Herakles stripped him of life and limb   290
By his shambling cattle on sea-circled Erythea
The day he drove those broadfaced cattle away
To holy Tiryns, crossing the ford of Ocean
And killing Orthos and the herdsman Eurytion
In that hazy stead beyond glorious Ocean.   295

And she bore another monster, irresistible,
Not like mortal men at all, or immortal gods,
Bore it in a hollow cave, divine brutal Echidna:
Half dancing-eyed nymph with pretty cheeks,
Half horrible serpent, an iridescent monster   300
Eating raw flesh in sacred earth's dark crypts.
Her cave is deep undergound in the hollow rock
Far from mortal men and from immortal gods,
Her glorious home, and there she keeps guard
In underground Arima, grim Echidna,   305
A nymph immortal and all her days ageless.

This nymph with dancing eyes mated, they say,
With dreadnaught Typhaon, willful and wild,

Got pregnant and bore him a brutal brood.
310   First she bore Orthos, Geryones' hound.
Second, a monster that beggars description
The carnivore Cerberos, Hades' bronze-baying hound,
Fifty-headed and an irresistible force.
And third, a Hydra, malicious and grisly,
315   The Lernaean Hydra that the white-armed goddess
Hera nourished, infinitely peeved with Herakles,
The son of Zeus (but of the house of Amphitryon)
Who used merciless bronze to despoil the monster
With Iolaos' help and Athena's strategy.

320   And she bore Chimaira, who breathed raging fire,
And she was dreadful and huge and fast and strong
And she had three heads: one of a green-eyed lion,
One of a goat, and one of a serpent, a gnarly dragon
(Lion in front, dragon in the rear, goat in the middle)
325   And every exhalation was a breath of pure flame.
Pegasos did her in, and noble Bellerophon.

She was the mother of Sphinx, the deadly destroyer
Of Cadmos' descendants, after mating with Orthos,
And of the Nemean Lion, that Zeus' dutiful wife
330   Hera raised, to roam and ravage Nemea's hills,
A spectral killer that destroyed whole villages,
Master of Nemean Tretos and Apesas.
But Herakles muscled him down in the end.

And Keto mingled in love with Phorkys
335   And bore her youngest, the dreaded serpent
Who guards the apples of solid gold
In the dark earth's crypts at its vast outer limits,
And is last of the offspring of Keto and Phorkys.

And Tethys bore to Ocean eddying rivers:

340   Nilos, Alpheios, and Eridanos swirling,
Strymon, Maiandros, and Istros streaming,
Phasis, Rhesos, and Akheloos silvery,
Nessos, Rhodios, Haliakmon, Heptaporon,

Granikos, Aisepos, and holy Simois,
Peneios, Hermos, and lovely Kaikos,   *345*
Sangarios the great, Parthenios and Ladon,
Euenos, Ardeskos and divine Skamandros.

And she bore as well a holy brood of daughters
Who work with Apollo and with the Rivers
To make boys into men. Zeus gave them this charge.   *350*

Peitho, Admete, Ianthe, Elektra,
Doris, Prymno, and godlike Ourania,
Hippo, Klymene, Rhodeia, Kallirhoe,
Zeuxo, Klytie, Idyia, Pasithoe,
Plexaure, Galaxuare, lovely Dione,   *355*
Melobosis, Thoe, and fair Polydore,
Shapely Kerkeis, and cow-eyed Plouto,
Perseis, Ianeira, Akaste and Xanthe,
Beautiful Petraia, Menestho, Europa,
Metis, Eurynome, and Telesto in saffron,   *360*
Chryseis, Asia, desirable Kalypso,
Eudora and Tykhe, Amphiro and Okyroe,
And Styx, who is most important of all.

These are Ocean's and Tethys' eldest daughters,
But there are many more besides, three thousand   *365*
Slender-ankled Ocean nymphs scattered everywhere
Haunting earth and deep waters, offspring divine.
And as many other rivers, chattering as they flow,
Sons of Ocean that Lady Tethys bore,
But it is hard for a mortal to tell all their names.   *370*
People know the rivers near which they dwell.

And Theia bore great Helios and glowing Selene
And Eos, Dawn, who shines for all upon earth
And for the immortals who possess the wide sky,
After Theia was mastered by Hyperion in love.   *375*

And Eurybia mingled in love with Krios,
And the bright goddess bore great Astraios and Pallas,
And Perses, who was pre-eminent in wisdom.

And Dawn bore to Astraios the mighty Winds,
380   Silverwhite Zephyros and onrushing Boreas,
And Notos, after the goddess slept with the god.
Then the Early-born Goddess bore the Dawnstar
And the other shining stars that crown the sky.

And Styx, Ocean's daughter, made love with Pallas
385   And bore Vying in her house and beautiful Victory,
And Strength and Force—notable children she bore,
And they have no house apart from Zeus, no dwelling
Or path except where the god leads them,
And they dwell forever with deep-thundering Zeus.
390   For this was how Styx, Ocean's undying daughter,
Made her decision on that fateful day
When the Lord of Lightning summoned the gods
To the slopes of Olympos, and told them whoever
Fought along with him against the Titans
395   He would not deprive of any rights and honors
Among the deathless gods, or if they had none
Under Kronos before, he would promote them
To rights and honors, as was only just.
And Styx undying was first to come to Olympos
400   Along with her children, her beloved father's idea.
And Zeus honored her and gave her extraordinary gifts,
Made her what the gods swear their great oaths by,
And decreed her children would live forever with him.
And what he promised to all of them he absolutely
405   Accomplished, but he himself has the power and rules.

And Phoibe came to Koios, and in the sensual embrace
Of the god she loved the goddess became pregnant
And bore Leto, robed in midnight blue, gentle always,
Mild to mortal men and to immortal gods,
410   Gentle from the beginning, the kindest being on Olympos.
And she bore auspicious Asteria, whom Perses once
Led to his house to be called his dear wife.
And she bore Hekate, whom Zeus son of Kronos
Has esteemed above all and given splendid gifts,
415   A share of the earth as her own, and of the barren sea.
She has received a province of starry heaven as well,

And is most highly esteemed by the deathless gods.
For even now when any man upon earth
Sacrifices and prays according to ancestral rites
He calls upon Hekate and is greatly blessed   420
If the goddess propitiously receives his prayers,
And riches come to him, for she has the power.
She has a share of the privileges of all the gods
That were ever born of Earth and Heaven.
Nor did Kronos' Son violate or reduce   425
What she had from the earlier gods, the Titans.
She keeps what she had in the primeval allotment.
Nor does the goddess, since she is an only child,
Have any less privilege on earth, sea, or heaven,
But all the more, since Zeus privileges her.   430
Whom she will, she greatly aids and advances,
And makes preeminent in the assembly,
And she sits beside reverend kings in judgment.
And when men arm themselves for devastating war
The goddess is at their sides, ready to give victory   435
And bestow glory upon whomever she will,
Good at standing by horsemen she wishes to help.
When men compete in athletic contests
The goddess stands by them too, knows how to help,
And the triumphant victor wins a beautiful prize   440
For his prowess and strength, and praise for his parents.
And those who work the surly grey sea
Pray to Hekate and the booming Earthshaker,
And the goddess easily sends a big catch their way,
Or removes one in sight, as she wills in her heart.   445
She is good, with Hermes, at increasing stock in a pen,
Droves of cattle, herds of goats on a plain,
Flocks of wooly sheep—if she wills in her heart
She can multiply them or make them diminish.
And so although she is her mother's only child,   450
She is a privileged goddess among the Immortals.
And the Son of Kronos made her a nurse of the young
Who from that day on saw with their eyes
The light of Dawn that sees all. So from the beginning
She is a nurse of the young. These are Hekate's honors.   455

The Birth of the Olympians

Later, Kronos forced himself upon Rheia,
And she gave birth to a splendid brood:

Hestia and Demeter and gold-sandalled Hera,
Strong, pitiless Hades, the underworld lord,
460   The booming Earth-shaker, Poseidon, and finally
Zeus, a wise god, our Father in heaven
Under whose thunder the wide world trembles.

And Kronos swallowed them all down as soon as each
Issued from Rheia's holy womb onto her knees,
465   With the intent that only he among the proud Ouranians
Should hold the title of King among the Immortals.
For he had learned from Earth and starry Heaven
That it was fated for him, powerful though he was,
To be overthrown by his child, through the scheming of Zeus.
470   Well, Kronos wasn't blind. He kept a sharp watch
And swallowed his children.
                    Rheia's grief was unbearable.
When she was about to give birth to Zeus our Father
She petitioned her parents, Earth and starry Heaven,
475   To put together some plan so that the birth of her child
Might go unnoticed, and she would make devious Kronos
Pay the Avengers of her father and children.
They listened to their daughter and were moved by her words,
And the two of them told her all that was fated
480   For Kronos the King and his stout-hearted son.
They sent her to Lyktos, to the rich land of Crete,
When she was ready to bear the youngest of her sons,
Mighty Zeus. Vast Earth received him when he was born
To be nursed and brought up in the wide land of Crete.
485   She came first to Lyktos, travelling quickly by night,
And took the baby in her hands and hid him in a cave,
An eerie hollow in the woods of dark Mount Aigaion.
Then she wrapped up a great stone in swaddling clothes
And gave it to Kronos, Ouranos' son, the great lord and king
490   Of the earlier gods. He took it in his hands and rammed it
Down into his belly, the poor fool! He had no idea

That a stone had been substituted for his son, who,
Unscathed and content as a babe, would soon wrest
His honors from him by main force and rule the Immortals.
It wasn't long before the young lord was flexing 495
His glorious muscles. The seasons followed each other,
And great devious Kronos, gulled by Earth's
Clever suggestions, vomited up his offspring,
[Overcome by the wiles and power of his son]
The stone first, which he'd swallowed last. 500
Zeus took the stone and set it in the ground at Pytho
Under Parnassos' hollows, a sign and wonder for men to come.
And he freed his uncles, other sons of Ouranos
Whom their father in a fit of idiocy had bound.
They remembered his charity and in gratitude 505
Gave him thunder and the flashing thunderbolt
And lightning, which enormous Earth had hidden before.
Trusting in these he rules mortals and Immortals.

Prometheus

Then Iapetos led away a daughter of Ocean,
Klymene, pretty ankles, and went to bed with her. 510
And she bore him a child, Atlas, stout heart,
And begat ultraglorious Menoitios, and Prometheus,
Complex, his mind a shimmer, and witless Epimetheus,
Who was trouble from the start for enterprising men,
First to accept from Zeus the fabricated woman, 515
The Maiden. Outrageous Menoitios broadbrowed Zeus
Blasted into Erebos with a sulphurous thunderbolt
On account of his foolishness and excessive violence.
Atlas, crimped hard, holds up the wide sky
At earth's limits, in front of the shrill-voiced Hesperides, 520
Standing with indefatigable head and hands,
For this is the part wise Zeus assigned him.
And he bound Prometheus with ineluctable fetters,
Painful bonds, and drove a shaft through his middle,
And set a long-winged eagle on him that kept gnawing 525
His undying liver, but whatever the long-winged bird
Ate the whole day through, would all grow back by night.
That bird the mighty son of pretty-ankled Alkmene,

Herakles, killed, drove off the evil affliction
530   From Iapetos' son and freed him from his misery—
Not without the will of Zeus, high lord of Olympos,
So that the glory of Theban-born Herakles
Might be greater than before on the plentiful earth.
He valued that and honored his celebrated son.
535   And he ceased from the anger that he had before
Because Prometheus matched wits with mighty Kronion.

That happened when the gods and mortal men were negotiating
At Mekone. Prometheus cheerfully butchered a great ox
And served it up, trying to befuddle Zeus' wits.
540   For Zeus he set out flesh and innards rich with fat
Laid out on the oxhide and covered with its paunch.
But for the others he set out the animal's white bones
Artfully dressed out and covered with shining fat.
And then the Father of gods and men said to him:

545   "Son of Iapetos, my celebrated lord,
How unevenly you have divided the portions."

Thus Zeus, sneering, with imperishable wisdom.
And Prometheus, whose mind was devious,
Smiled softly and remembered his trickery:

550   "Zeus most glorious, greatest of the everlasting gods,
Choose whichever of these your heart desires."

This was Prometheus' trick. But Zeus, eternally wise,
Recognized the fraud and began to rumble in his heart
Trouble for mortals, and it would be fulfilled.
555   With both his hands he picked up the gleaming fat.
Anger seethed in his lungs and bile rose to his heart
When he saw the ox's white bones artfully tricked out.
And that is why the tribes of men on earth
Burn white bones to the immortals upon smoking altars.
560   But cloudherding Zeus was terribly put out, and said:

"Iapetos' boy, if you're not the smartest of them all.
So you still haven't forgotten your tricks, have you?"

Thus Zeus, angry, whose wisdom never wears out.
From then on he always remembered this trick
And wouldn't give the power of weariless fire   *565*
To the ashwood mortals who live on the earth.
But that fine son of Iapetos outwitted him
And stole the far-seen gleam of weariless fire
In a hollow fennel stalk, and so bit deeply the heart
Of Zeus, the high lord of thunder, who was angry   *570*
When he saw the distant gleam of fire among men,
And straight off he gave them trouble to pay for the fire.

Pandora

The famous Lame God plastered up some clay
To look like a shy virgin, just like Zeus wanted,
And Athena, the Owl-Eyed Goddess,   *575*
Got her all dressed up in silvery clothes
And with her hands draped a veil from her head,
An intricate thing, wonderful to look at.
And Pallas Athena circled her head
With a wreath of luscious springtime flowers   *580*
And crowned her with a golden tiara
That the famous Lame God had made himself,
Shaped it by hand to please father Zeus,
Intricately designed and a wonder to look at.
Sea monsters and other fabulous beasts   *585*
Crowded the surface, and it sighed with beauty,
And you could almost hear the animals' voices.

He made this lovely evil to balance the good,
Then led her off to the other gods and men
Gorgeous in the finery of the owl-eyed daughter   *590*
Sired in power. And they were stunned,
Immortal gods and mortal men, when they saw
The sheer deception, irresistible to men.
From her is the race of female women,
The deadly race and population of women,   *595*
A great infestation among mortal men,
At home with Wealth but not with Poverty.
It's the same as with bees in their overhung hives

Feeding the drones, evil conspirators.
600   The bees work every day until the sun goes down,
Busy all day long making pale honeycombs,
While the drones stay inside, in the hollow hives,
Stuffing their stomachs with the work of others.
That's just how Zeus, the high lord of thunder,
605   Made women as a curse for mortal men,
Evil conspirators. And he added another evil
To offset the good. Whoever escapes marriage
And women's harm, comes to deadly old age
Without any son to support him. He has no lack
610   While he lives, but when he dies distant relatives
Divide up his estate. Then again, whoever marries
As fated, and gets a good wife, compatible,
Has a life that is balanced between evil and good,
A constant struggle. But if he marries the abusive kind,
615   He lives with pain in his heart all down the line,
Pain in spirit and mind, incurable evil.
There's no way to get around the mind of Zeus.
Not even Prometheus, that fine son of Iapetos
Escaped his heavy anger. He knows many things,
620   But he is caught in the crimp of ineluctable bonds.

The Titanomachy

When their father Ouranus first grew angry
With Obriareus, and with his brothers,
Kottos and Gyges, he clamped down on them hard.
Indignant because of their arrogant maleness,
625   Their looks and bulk, he made them live underground.
So there they lived in subterranean pain,
Settled at the outermost limits of earth,
Suffering long and hard, grief in their hearts.
But the Son of Kronos, and the other Immortals
630   Born of Rheia and Kronos, took Earth's advice
And led them up back into the light, for she
Told them the whole story of how with their help
They would win glorious honor and victory.

For a long time they fought, hearts bitter with toil,

Going against each other in the shock of battle, 635
The Titans and the gods who were born from Kronos.
The proud Titans fought from towering Othrys,
And from Olympos the gods, the givers of good
Born of rich-haired Rheia after lying with Kronos.
They battled each other with pain in their hearts 640
Continuously for ten full years, never a truce,
No respite from the hostilities on either side,
The war's outcome balanced between them.
Then Zeus gave those three all that they needed
Of ambrosia and nectar, food the gods themselves eat, 645
And the fighting spirit grew in their breasts
When they fed on the sweet ambrosia and nectar.
Then the father of gods and men addressed them:

"Hear me, glorious children of Earth and Heaven,
While I speak my mind. For a long time now 650
The Titans and those of us born from Kronos
Have been fighting daily for victory and dominance.
Show the Titans your strength, the invincible might
Of your hands, oppose them in this grisly conflict
Remembering our kindness. After suffering so much 655
You have come back to the light from your cruel dungeon,
Returned by my will from the moldering gloom."

Thus Zeus, and the blameless Kottos replied:

"Divine One, what a thing to say. We already realize
That your thoughts are supreme, your mind surpassing, 660
That you saved the Immortals from war's cold light.
We have come from under the moldering gloom
By your counsel, free at last from bonds none too gentle,
O Lord, Son of Kronos, and from suffering unlooked for.
Our minds are bent therefore, and our wills fixed 665
On preserving your power through the horror of war.
We will fight the Titans in the crush of battle."

He spoke, and the gods who are givers of good
Heard him and cheered, and their hearts yearned for war
Even more than before. They joined grim battle again 670

That very day, all of them, male and female alike,
The Titans and the gods who were born from Kronos,
And the three Zeus sent from the underworld to light,
Dread and strong, and arrogant with might.
675   A hundred hands stuck out of their shoulders,
Grotesque, and fifty heads grew on each stumpy neck.
They stood against the Titans on the line of battle
Holding chunks of cliffs in their rugged hands.
Opposite them, the Titans tightened their ranks
680   Expectantly. Then both sides' hands flashed with power,
And the unfathomable sea shrieked eerily,
The earth crashed and rumbled, the vast sky groaned
And quavered, and massive Olympos shook from its roots
Under the Immortals' onslaught. A deep tremor of feet
685   Reached misty Tartaros, and a high whistling noise
Of insuppressible tumult and heavy missiles
That groaned and whined in flight. And the sound
Of each side shouting rose to starry heaven,
As they collided with a magnificent battle cry.

690   And now Zeus no longer held back his strength.
His lungs seethed with anger and he revealed
All his power. He charged from the sky, hurtling
Down from Olympos in a flurry of lightning,
Hurling thunderbolts one after another, right on target,
695   From his massive hand, a whirlwind of holy flame.
And the earth that bears life roared as it burned,
And the endless forests crackled in fire,
The continents melted and the Ocean streams boiled,
And the barren sea. The blast of heat enveloped
700   The chthonian Titans, and the flame reached
The bright stratosphere, and the incandescent rays
Of the thunderbolts and lightning flashes
Blinded their eyes, mighty as they were,
Heat so terrible it engulfed deep Chaos.
705   The sight of it all
And its sound to the ears was just as if broad Heaven
Had fallen on Earth: the noise of it crashing
And of Earth being crushed would be like the noise
That arose from the strife of the clashing gods.

Winds hissed through the earth, starting off tremors 710
And swept dust and thunder and flashing bolts of lightning,
The weapons of Zeus, along with the shouting and din,
Into both sides. Reverberation from the terrible strife
Hung in the air, and sheer Power shone through it.

And the battle turned. Before they had fought 715
Shoulder to shoulder in the crush of battle,
But then Kottos, Briareos, and Gyges rallied,
Hungry for war, in the front lines of combat,
Firing three hundred stones one after the other
From their massive hands, and the stones they shot 720
Overshadowed the Titans, and they sent them under
The wide-pathed earth and bound them with cruel bonds—
Having beaten them down despite their daring—
As far under earth as the sky is above,
For it is that far from earth down to misty Tartaros. 725

Tartaros

A bronze anvil falling down from the sky
Would fall nine days and nights and on the tenth hit earth.
It is just as far from earth down to misty Tartaros.
A bronze anvil falling down from earth
Would fall nine days and nights and on the tenth hit Tartaros. 730
There is a bronze wall beaten round it, and Night
In a triple row flows round its neck, while above it grow
The roots of earth and the unharvested sea.

There the Titans are concealed in the misty gloom
By the will of Zeus who gathers the clouds, 735
In a moldering place, the vast earth's limits.
There is no way out for them. Poseidon set doors
Of bronze in a wall that surrounds it.
There Gyges and Kottos and stouthearted Briareos
Have their homes, the trusted guards of the Storm King, Zeus. 740

There dark Earth and misty Tartaros
And the barren Sea and the starry Sky
All have their sources and limits in a row,
Grim and dank, which even the gods abhor.
The gaping hole is immense. A man could not reach bottom 745

In a year's time—if he ever got through the gates—
But wind after fell wind would blow him about.
It is terrible even for the immortal gods,
Eerie and monstrous. And the house of black Night
750   Stands forbidding and shrouded in dark blue clouds.

In front the son of Iapetos supports the wide sky
With his head and indefatigable hands, standing
Immobile, where Night and Day greet each other
As they pass over the great threshold of bronze.
755   One goes down inside while the other goes out,
And the house never holds both inside together,
But one of them is always outside the house
And traverses the earth while the other remains
Inside the house until her journey's hour has come.
760   One holds for earthlings the far-seeing light;
The other holds Death's brother, Sleep, in her arms:
Night the destroyer, shrouded in fog and mist.

There the children of black Night have their house,
Sleep and Death, awesome gods. Never does Helios
765   Glowing in his rays look upon these two
When he ascends the sky or from the sky descends.
One roams the earth and the wide back of the sea,
A quiet spirit, and is gentle to humans;
The other's heart is iron, unfeeling bronze,
770   And when he catches a man he holds on to him.
He is hateful even to the immortal gods.

In front of that stand the echoing halls
Of mighty Hades and dread Persephone,
Underworld gods, and a frightful, pitiless
775   Hound stands guard, and he has a mean trick:
When someone comes in he fawns upon him
Wagging his tail and dropping his ears,
But he will not allow anyone to leave—
He runs down and eats anyone he catches
780   Leaving Persephone's and Hades' gates.

And there dwells a goddess loathed by the Immortals,

Awesome Styx, eldest daughter of back-flowing Ocean.
She lives in a glorious house apart from the gods,
Roofed in towering stone, surrounded on all sides
With silver columns that reach up to the sky.   *785*
Seldom does Iris, Thaumas' swift-footed daughter,
Come bearing a message over the sea's wide back.
Whenever discord and strife arise among the gods,
Or any who have homes on Olympos should lie,
Zeus sends Iris to bring the gods' great oath   *790*
Back from afar in a golden pitcher, the celebrated water
That trickles down cold from precipitous stone.
Far underneath the wide-pathed earth it flows
From the holy river through midnight black,
A branch of Ocean, allotted a tenth of its waters.   *795*
Nine parts circle earth and the sea's broad back
In silvery currents returning to Ocean's brine.
But one part flows from stone, woe to the gods.
If ever a god who lives on snowcapped Olympos
Pours a libation of this and breaks his oath,   *800*
He lies a full year without any breath,
Not a taste of ambrosia, not a sip of nectar
Comes to his lips, but he lies breathless and speechless
On a blanketed bed, an evil coma upon him.
But when the long year brings this disease to its end,   *805*
Another more difficult trial is in store,
Nine years of exile from the everlasting gods,
No converse in council or at their feasts
For nine full years. In the tenth year finally
He rejoins the Immortals in their homes on Olympos.   *810*
Upon this the gods swear, the primordial, imperishable
Water of Styx, and it issues from a forbidding place.

There dark Earth and misty Tartaros
And the barren Sea and the starry Sky
All have their sources and limits in a row,   *815*
Grim and dank, which even the gods abhor.
There are shining gates and a bronze threshhold,
Deeply rooted and firmly fixed, a natural
Outgrowth. Beyond and far from all the gods
The Titans dwell, past the gloom of Chaos.   *820*

But the famous helpers of thunderous Zeus
Inhabit houses on Ocean's deep fundaments,
Kottos and Gyges. And Briareos for his bravery
Deep-booming Poseidon made his son-in-law,
825   And gave him Kymopoleia in marriage.

Typhoios

When Zeus had driven the Titans from heaven,
                  Earth,
Pregnant by Tartaros thanks to golden Aphrodite,
Delivered her last-born child, Typhoios,
830   A god whose hands were like engines of war,
Whose feet never gave out, from whose shoulders grew
The hundred heads of a frightful dragon
Flickering dusky tongues, and the hollow eyesockets
In the eerie heads sent out fiery rays,
835   And each head burned with flame as it glared.
And there were voices in each of these frightful heads,
A phantasmagoria of unspeakable sound,
Sometimes sounds that the gods understood, sometimes
The sound of a spirited bull, bellowing and snorting,
840   Or the uninhibited, shameless roar of a lion,
Or just like puppies yapping, an uncanny noise,
Or a whistle hissing through long ridges and hills.
And that day would have been beyond hope of help,
And Typhoios would have ruled over Immortals and men,
845   Had the father of both not been quick to notice.
He thundered hard, and the Earth all around
Rumbled horribly, and wide Heaven above,
The Sea, the Ocean, and underground Tartaros.
Great Olympos trembled under the deathless feet
850   Of the Lord as he rose, and Gaia groaned.
The heat generated by these two beings—
Scorching winds from Zeus' lightning bolts
And the monster's fire—enveloped the violet sea.
Earth, sea, and sky were a seething mass,
855   And long tidal waves from the immortals' impact
Pounded the beaches, and a quaking arose that would not stop.
Hades, lord of the dead below, trembled,

And the Titans under Tartaros huddled around Kronos,
At the unquenchable clamor and fearsome strife.
When Zeus' temper had peaked he seized his weapons,   *860*
Searing bolts of thunder and lightning,
And as he leaped from Olympos, struck. He burned
All the eerie heads of the frightful monster,
And when he had beaten it down he whipped it until
It reeled off maimed, and vast Earth groaned.   *865*
And a firestorm from the thunderstricken lord
Spread through the dark rugged glens of the mountain,
And a blast of hot vapor melted the earth like tin
When smiths use bellows to heat it in crucibles,
Or like iron, the hardest substance there is,   *870*
When it is softened by fire in mountain glens
And melts in bright earth under Hephaistos' hands.
So the earth melted in the incandescent flame.
And in anger Zeus hurled him into Tartaros' pit.

And from Typhoios come the damp monsoons,   *875*
But not Notos, Boreas, or silverwhite Zephyros.
These winds are godsent blessings to men,
But the others blow fitfully over the water,
Evil gusts falling on the sea's misty face,
A great curse for mortals, raging this way and that,   *880*
Scattering ships and destroying sailors—no defense
Against those winds when men meet them at sea.
And others blow over endless, flowering earth
Ruining beautiful farmlands of sod-born humans,
Filling them with dust and howling rubble.   *885*

Zeus in Power

So the blessed gods had done a hard piece of work,
Settled by force the question of rights with the Titans.
Then at Gaia's suggestion they pressed broad-browed Zeus,
The Olympian, to be their king and rule the Immortals.
And so Zeus dealt out their privileges and rights.   *890*

Now king of the gods, Zeus made Metis his first wife,
Wiser than any other god, or any mortal man.

But when she was about to deliver the owl-eyed goddess
Athena, Zeus tricked her, gulled her with crafty words,
895   And stuffed her in his stomach, taking the advice
Of Earth and starry Heaven. They told him to do this
So that no one but Zeus would hold the title of King
Among the eternal gods, for it was predestined
That very wise children would be born from Metis,
900   First the grey-eyed girl, Tritogeneia,
Equal to her father in strength and wisdom,
But then a son with an arrogant heart
Who would one day be king of gods and men.
But Zeus stuffed the goddess into his stomach first
905   So she would devise with him good and evil both.

Next he married gleaming Themis, who bore the Seasons,
And Eunomia, Dike, and blooming Eirene,
Who attend to mortal men's works for them,
And the Moirai, whom wise Zeus gave honor supreme:
910   Klotho, Lakhesis, and Atropos, who assign
To mortal men the good and evil they have.

And Ocean's beautiful daughter Eurynome
Bore to him the three rose-cheeked Graces,
Aglaia, Euphrosyne, and lovely Thalia.
915   The light from their eyes melts limbs with desire,
One beautiful glance from under their brows.

And he came to the bed of bountiful Demeter,
Who bore white-armed Persephone, stolen by Hades
From her mother's side. But wise Zeus gave her away.

920   And he made love to Mnemosyne with beautiful hair,
From whom nine Muses with golden diadems were born,
And their delight is in festivals and the pleasures of song.

And Leto bore Apollo and arrowy Artemis,
The loveliest brood of all the Ouranians
925   After mingling in love with Zeus Aegisholder.

Last of all Zeus made Hera his blossoming wife,

And she gave birth to Hebe, Eileithyia, and Ares,
After mingling in love with the lord of gods and men.

From his own head he gave birth to owl-eyed Athena,
The awesome, battle-rousing, army-leading, untiring   *930*
Lady, whose pleasure is fighting and the metallic din of war.
And Hera, furious at her husband, bore a child
Without making love, glorious Hephaistos,
The finest artisan of all the Ouranians.

From Amphitrite and the booming Earthshaker   *935*
Mighty Triton was born, who with his dear mother
And kingly father lives in a golden palace
In the depths of the sea, an awesome divinity.

And Aphrodite bore to shield-piercing Ares
Phobos and Deimos, awesome gods who rout   *940*
Massed ranks of soldiers with pillaging Ares
In icy war. And she bore Harmonia also,
Whom high-spirited Kadmos made his wife.

The Atlantid Maia climbed into Zeus' sacred bed
And bore glorious Hermes, the Immortals' herald.   *945*

And Kadmos' daughter Semele bore to Zeus
A splendid son after they mingled in love,
Laughing Dionysos, a mortal woman
Giving birth to a god. But they are both divine now.

And Alkmene gave birth to the might of Herakles   *950*
After mingling in love with cloud-herding Zeus.

And Hephaistos the glorious Lame God married
Blossoming Aglaia, youngest of the Graces.

Gold-haired Dionysos made blond Ariadne,
Minos' daughter, his blossoming wife,   *955*
And Kronion made her deathless and ageless.

And Herakles, Alkmene's mighty son,

Finished with all his agonizing labors,
Made Hebe his bride on snowy Olympos,
960   Daughter of Zeus and gold-sandalled Hera.
Happy at last, his great work done, he lives
Agelessly and at ease among the Immortals.

To tireless Helios the glorious Oceanid,
Perseis, bore Kirke and Aietes the king.
965   Aietes, son of Helios who shines on mortals,
Wed fair-cheeked Idyia by the gods' designs,
Daughter of Ocean, the perfect river,
And she bore Medeia with her well-turned ankles
After she was mastered in love, thanks to golden Aphrodite.

Goddesses and Heroes

970   And now farewell, all you Olympians,
You islands and mainlands and salt sea between.
Now sing of the goddesses, Olympian Muses,
Wordsweet daughters of Zeus Aegisholder—
The goddesses who slept with mortal men,
975   And immortal themselves bore children like gods.

Demeter bore Ploutos after the shining goddess
Had made sweet love to the hero Iasion
In a thrice-ploughed field in the rich land of Crete.
Her good son travels all over land and sea,
980   And into whosoever hands he falls, whoever he meets,
He makes that man rich and bestows great wealth upon him.

And Harmonia, daughter of golden Aphrodite,
Bore to Kadmos Ino and Semele
And fair-cheeked Agaue and Autonoe,
985   Whom deep-haired Aristaios wed,
And Polydoros in Thebes crowned with towers.

And Ocean's daughter Kallirhoe mingled in love
Of Aphrodite golden with stout-hearted Chrysaor
And bore him a son, of all mortals the strongest,
990   Geryones, whom the might of Herakles killed

For his shambling cattle on wave-washed Erytheia.

And Dawn bore to Tithonos bronze-helmeted Memnon,
The Ethiopian king, and the Lord Emathion.
And for Kephalos she produced a splendid son,
Powerful Phaethon, a man in the gods' image.   *995*
When he was a boy in the tender bloom of youth,
Still childish in mind, Aphrodite rose smiling
And snatched him away and made him a keeper
Of her holy shrine by night, a spirit divine.

And Jason son of Aison led off from Aietes,   *1000*
A king fostered by Zeus, Aietes' daughter,
By the eternal gods' will, after he completed
The many hard labors the outrageously arrogant,
Presumptuous bully, King Pelias, set for him.
The son of Aison suffered through the labors   *1005*
And sailed to Iolkos with the dancing-eyed girl
And made her his wife, and in her bloom
She was mastered by Jason, shepherd of his people,
And bore a child, Medeios, whom the centaur Chiron
Phillyrides raised in the hills. And Zeus' will was done.   *1010*

Of the daughters of Nereus, the Old Man of the Sea,
The bright goddess Psamathe bore Phokos to Aiakos,
Out of love for him through golden Aphrodite.
And silver-footed Thetis was mastered by Peleus
And bore Akhilles, the lion-hearted killer of men.   *1015*

And Kythereia, beautifully crowned, bore Aineias,
After mingling in sweet love with the hero Ankhises
On the peaks above Ida's many wooded glens.

And Circe, daughter of Hyperion's son Helios,
Loved enduring Odysseus and bore to him   *1020*
Agrios and Latinos, faultless and strong,
And bore Telegonos through golden Aphrodite.
In a far off corner of the holy islands
They ruled over all the famous Tyrsenians.
And the bright goddess Kalypso bore to Odysseus   *1025*

Nausithoos and Nausinoos after making sweet love.

These are the goddesses who slept with mortal men,
And immortal themselves bore children like gods.

Now sing of the women, Olympian Muses,
1030   Wordsweet daughters of Zeus Aegisholder. . . .

End of Theogony

NOTES: *THEOGONY*

1–115 [1–115] The prologue or proem of the *Theogony* is a great deal longer and more elaborate than that of the *Works and Days*. Along with the passage on seafaring in the *Works and Days*, the two prologues are the parts of the Hesiodic corpus in which the poet is defined and his Boeotian home evoked. All three passages also evoke the Muses and bind the poetry to the context of their precinct near Helikon, the site of the festival known as the Mouseia. In the *Works and Days* they are called from Pieria, north of Mt. Olympos, but here it is specifically the Helikonian cult that Hesiod takes as his point of departure, though they are called "Olympian" repeatedly elsewhere in the prologue.

5–6 [5–6] *Permessos, Olmeios, Horse Spring:* The topography of the valley northwest of Thespiai in western Boeotia where the Muses' festival was celebrated can be made to fit quite nicely with the toponyms provided in the poems. There are two streams, presumably the Permessos and the Olmeios, that come together near the site of a large village, abandoned in antiquity, a likely candidate for Askra. The "Horse Spring" (Hippokrene) is identified with a remarkable well with ancient blocks, about a half day's climb above the valley and the precinct of the Muses, high on a spur of Helikon.

23–35 [22–34] The Muses' gift of laurel to the shepherd Hesiod is the first representation of the initiation of the poet in European literature and has had a very rich history of imitation and adaptation. The choice of laurel probably points to Apollo as leader of the Muses. His Delphic shrine was rich in laurel. These thirty-five lines establish the identification of the speaker of this poem with the highly individualized speaker of the *Works and Days*, but from this point on, that persona has little if any impact on the *Theogony*.

36 [35] *But why all this . . .:* The phrase was proverbial. Its exact sense here is impossible to recover, but it is striking that it marks the abandonment of the personalized persona of the shepherd of Helikon in this poem.

37 [36] *Start from the Muses:* The lengthy hymn to the Muses that serves as prologue to the *Theogony* is the principal link between the Hesiodic corpus and the cult and festival of the Muses located in a valley of Mt. Helikon, west of Thespiai in Boeotia.

39 [38] *Telling what is . . .:* The same phrase is used in the *Iliad* (1.70) to describe the range of the mind of the seer Calchas.

45 [42] ff. The Muses are evoked as singers of their own *Theogony* for the Olympians.

54 [54] *Memory*: Although Hesiod finds a place for Mnemosyne in his generational scheme (135 [135]), she has no cult or mythology beyond her role here, and so can be taken as an essentially allegorical figure, a personification rather than a fully developed deity.

73 [72] *vajra thunder*: In Vedic mythology, the *vajra* is the weapon of the thunder-god Indra. There is no explicit reference to that tradition in the Greek text, but there is no doubt that the Vedas represent an Indo-European tradition of theology and of epic song parallel to what we find in early Greek poetry.

78–80 [77–79] *Klio*, etc.: This, the canonical list of the names of the nine Muses, is in all probability the invention of the Hesiodic tradition of poetry. The names are descriptive (e.g. Kalliope = "pretty voice"). The assignment of specific roles to each Muse (e.g. Kalliope = the muse of epic poetry) is not Hesiodic and presumably represents a later development.

85 [84] *words flow like honey*: Eloquence is the link between the Muses and the good ruler, whose principal roles in Hesiod's view are arbitration and the righting of wrongs. The parallel self-advertisement of the tradition of song that follows identifies bard and king as special beneficiaries of the gifts of the Muses.

105 [104] *Farewell . . .*: The poet closes the hymnic prologue by asking the Muses in effect to sing their account of the generations of the gods through *him*, making available to mankind what they offer directly to the gods on Olympos.

116 [116] *Chaos*. The word occurs first here, and rather than a "jumbled mass" or "confusion" (senses attached to the word in English), refers properly to a "gaping" or opening up of a space or abyss.

117–20 [117–20] *Gaia . . . Tartaros . . . Eros*: This first generation of gods might seem a strange grouping. That Earth should come first is perhaps obvious, but Tartaros, the region beyond Chaos, usually conceived as subterranean, will have no further function until the Titanomachy (see 814 [807]). Eros is the prerequisite for the genealogical model, and this presumably explains his unexpected primacy here.

123 [123] *Erebos and dark Night*: Probably to be understood as the darkness under the earth and the darkness above.

125 [125] *Aether and Day*: With the first light come also the first sexually generated offspring. Day (*hemere*) is seldom personified, but as the "days"

of the *Works and Days* bear witness, each day of the calendar has its own identity, and here (as in Genesis) a sort of generalized "day" precedes even the generation of the Sun (374 [371]), below.

126 [126–27] With Gaia's spontaneous generation, first of her principal consort Ouranos (Heaven), then of the mountains and the sea, the physical setting is largely complete and from this point on, the model of sexually generated generations is dominant.

131–37 [131–37] Sea (*pontos*) is less defined than Ocean, conceived as the river running around the world that ultimately receives the waters of all the rivers. Along with his five brothers and six sisters, he belongs to the first generation of sexually generated deities, known collectively as the Titans.

138–53 [139–55] After the Titans, Earth produces a series of monsters, all still fathered by Ouranos. Their roles here are somewhat anomalous. Ouranos shoves all his offspring back into their mother and confines them there, until the pattern is broken by Kronos. It seems that after Ouranos' castration the Titans themselves are released, but not these monsters, whom Zeus will free from an otherwise unexplained bondage later, when he needs them.

153–210 [154–210] The first distinct dramatic episode in the *Theogony*, the castration of Ouranos by Kronos, is emblematic of the violence of the primitive ages of the universe, before the imposition of the existing order by Zeus. Succession by castration is a feature of several much earlier Eastern creation stories, including the Hittite.

184–206 [183–206] The castration is not the end of Ouranos' career as a generating principle, since the spilled sperm impregnates Earth with the Furies, the Giants, and the Ash-tree Nymphs, and the genitals themselves (*medea*), floating in the sea, produce Aphrodite. Hence she is called *philommedes* (201 [200]) or "genital-loving"—an epithet that is commonly distorted into the prettier *philommeides* or "laughter-loving," which is presumably just a bowdlerization. This account of her birth is one of the striking instances of conflict between the Homeric and Hesiodic accounts of the origins of things: In Homer, Aphrodite is the daughter of Zeus and Dione.

207–10 [207–10] This etymology derives "Titan" from the verb *titaino*, which means "stretch" or "strain," perhaps with reference to Kronos' reaching out to castrate Ouranos, but the word play does not stop there— their name also contains a foretaste of the "vengeance" or "recompense" (*tisis*) that is in their future.

211–32 [211–32] From line 211 [211] down to the Prometheus story and Titanomachy (508 [507] ff.), the poem consists of a series of lists of the progeny of the primitive gods and the Titans. Night is first, and though she had originally produced Aether and Day after intercourse with her brother Erebos (124–25), she now generates a host of evils, all apparently fatherless, and then her daughter Eris ("strife") carries on to produce more. Most of these offspring are clearly rudimentary personifications, with transparent names and little or no story, but mixed in with such painful facts of human existence as Blame and Grief we find the Hesperides ("Daughters of the evening star") who guard the golden apples in a paradise in the West, as well as the Destinies (*keres*) and Fates (*moirai*). The Fates are given their traditional names for the first time here (though Homer has "spinners" (*Klothes*), to whom the Fate Clotho is clearly related). The description of the avenging deities (220–22 [220–22]) probably refers to the Keres rather than the Moirai. On Eris ("Strife") compare *Works and Days* 21 [11].

233–38 [233–36] After the sinister offspring of Night and Eris, we are given a list of the descendants of Pontos (Sea) and of his three sons, Nereus, Thaumas, and Phorkys. Two of these, Nereus and Thaumas, married daughters of Ocean (Electra and Doris), and the third, Phorkys, married his own sister Keto. The other daughter, Eurybia, married the Titan Krios (376 [375]), and the list of their descendants comes later.

233–65 [233–64] The list of the fifty daughters of Nereus, the Nereid Nymphs, may be dependent on the shorter list of Thetis' sisters who come to lament Patroclos in *Iliad* 18 (39–49). A few of them (Thetis herself, the mother of Achilles, and Amphitrite) had cults, but most probably did not. Many of the names are transparent: Erato = "Lovely" (also the name of one of the Muses), Psamathe = "Sea-sands," etc.

271–338 [270–336] Nereus' brothers Thaumas and Phorkys were less prolific, but each produced important groups of female divinities. Thaumas fathered the rapacious Harpies (who carry off the daughters of Pandareus in *Odyssey* 20.77, and in the story of the Argo spoil Phineas' meals), and Phorkys, the Graiai, and the Gorgons.

279 [278] *Dark-maned One*: Poseidon.

288–95 [287–94] The story of the birth of Chrysaor provides the opportunity for a capsule history of his three-headed son Geryon's demise at the hands of Herakles.

296 [295] *she*: Probably Keto (273 [270] above), so that this would be the

continuation of the progeny of Phorkys and Keto. The same problem arises at 322 [319] and 329 [326] below, where "she" could refer to any of several divinities in this disorderly genealogy of monsters.

305–26 [304–25] Echidna (mating with Earth's biggest and worst monster offspring, 826–85 [820–80] below) produces two monstrous dogs, Orthos and Cerberos, the Lernaean Hydra (a multiheaded snake of the marshlands of the Argolid), and finally (perhaps) the Chimaira, a composite creature eventually dispatched by the hero Bellerophon. The first three of her offspring all had run-ins with Herakles—Orthos and the Hydra, fatal ones.

327–33 [326–32] Chimaira is probably the mother of the Sphinx (or rather the "Phiks"—this local variant of "Sphinx" is the single example of Boeotian dialect in the Hesiodic corpus) and of the Nemean lion.

334–38 [333–36] Rounding off the descendants of Pontos, the poem returns to the generation of his children and the last child of Phorkys—the snake that guards the golden apples of the Hesperides (215 [215]) above.

339–620 [337–616] The central third of the poem concerns itself (with some narrative expansions) with the offspring of the Titans, the children of Ouranos and Gaia: Ocean and Tethys (339–72 [337–70]); Hyperion and Theia (372–75 [371–74]); Krios and Eurybia, the daughter of Pontos (376–405 [375–403]); Koios and Phoibe (406–55 [404–52]), including the Hekate hymn; then Kronos and Rhea (456–508 [453–506]), including the birth of Zeus; and finally Iapetos and the Oceanid Klymene (509–620 [507–616]), occupied largely by the Prometheus story.

339–72 [337–70] Of the myriad offspring of Oceanos and Tethys, Hesiod provides us with only a sample: twenty-five of the three thousand (male) rivers, and forty-one Oceanid Nymphs, again from a field of "three thousand." These compact lists of proper names blend together into a flow of evocative syllables—most of the river names might have been familiar to the ideal audience but for them as for us, few of these names could evoke anything but exotic fantasies, from the Nile to the Skamandros, flowing across the plain of Troy.

372–75 [371–74] That the Sun ("Helios") and Moon ("Selene") should come into existence so late in this theogony, long after "Day" (125 above, see n.) is rather strange. The fact that Helios' father, the Titan Hyperion ("he who passes over"), is identified with the Sun in Homer, may go some distance to explain the anomaly. But, more important, this is a reminder that this theogony is only casually and incidentally a cosmogony.

376–405 [375–403] The account of the obscure offspring of Krios and Eurybia continues the elaboration of the heavens. Their son Astraios ("starry") who mates with his cousin Dawn, to generate the stars, was probably invented for the purpose. The interesting story here antici- pates the Titanomachy (621 [617] ff.), which dominates the latter part of the *Theogony*. Krios' daughter-in-law, the Oceanid Styx, was the first to sign up to fight alongside Zeus, and in the distribution of honors, she became the oath of the gods (i.e. that by which the gods swear, and whatever binds the gods is in a sense the greatest power in the universe). She also brings to Olympos her offspring, personifications of "Vying," "Strength," "Force," and "Victory." Victory had her own cult in many places, and personified Strength and Force were sufficiently closely as- sociated with the rule of Zeus to serve as his agents in the binding of Prometheus in Aeschylus' *Prometheus Bound*.

382 [381] *The Early-born Goddess*: An epithet for Eos (Dawn).

406–55 [404–52] Koios and Phoibe produce only two daughters, Leto, later to be the mother of Apollo and Artemis (923 [918]), and Asteria, but the poem devotes some forty lines to Asteria's daughter Hekate. Various attempts have been made to account for the centrality of this celebration of Hekate in the *Theogony*. The extensive list of her honors is entirely out of scale with the treatment of other deities. Just as the story of Styx has pointed forward to the Titanomachy and the consolidation of Zeus' power, this episode (which immediately precedes the account of the offspring of Kronos and Rheia and the birth of Zeus) anticipates the benevolence and philanthropy of that new order that is soon to come. This is what is special about Hekate as she appears in this poem. She responds to prayers and provides all sorts of benefits for her devotees, from political prominence and military victory to a good catch of fish. With Hekate, mankind enters the poem, at least in anticipation, and we are given a sense for the first time of what all this means, from a human perspective. She also establishes a continuity with the past—she retains the honors she was given by the Titans—in contrast to Styx, who will rise to prominence with the new Olympian regime of Zeus.

413 [411] *And she bore Hekate*: That is, Asteria. Leto is thus the sister of Asteria, and Hekate the first cousin of Apollo and Artemis (Olympians richly intertwined in the lives of mortals).

449 [447] This capacity to cause increase or decrease is reminiscent of the primary attributes of Zeus in the prologue to the *Works and Days*.

456–508 [453–506] Among the offspring of the Titans, the most important, of course, are the Olympians, the older generation of whom are the children of Kronos and Rheia: Zeus, Hera, Poseidon, Hades, Demeter, and Hestia. Nowhere in the *Theogony* is the centrality of Zeus to this account of the universe clearer than it is here. His siblings are simply listed and remain passive. They would presumably have spent eternity in Kronos' gut, if Rheia had not found a way to save Zeus, and he, in turn, had not forced his father to vomit up his brothers and sisters. Hesiod tells us only that he accomplished this by using both his "wiles" and his "power" (499 [496]). He finally releases the Cyclopes from their captivity, imposed by Kronos, and, with the thunderbolts they provide, consolidates his power. This capsule account is echoed in the liberation of the Hundred-handers, below (621–33 [617–28]).

468–70 [463–65] The familiar motif of the oracle to the father warning him that he will be killed or overthrown by his son takes on a special force among the immortals, who cannot be disposed of in any simple way. The story turns on one of the tensions created by the application of a (human) succession myth to the generations of the gods. Note the difference from generation to generation: Kronos' father Ouranos used to shove his children back into their mother. Kronos removes her from the process and shoves them inside himself.

477–78 [472–73] *Avengers*: Ouranos' grievance for his castration entitles him to a Fury, and Zeus' older siblings, whose imprisonment likewise resembles a wrongful death, have theirs.

481 [477] *Crete*: Hesiod's account of the birth of Zeus in Crete seems to represent a conflation of a variety of traditions, including local Cretan ones.

501 [499] *Pytho*: Another name for Delphi.

503 [501] *his uncles*: The uncles in question must be the Cyclopes, who are the only ones who could supply him with thunderbolts. See 619–31 [617–29], where the imprisoned Hundred-handers are set free, and the incident is related in more detail. It is not absolutely certain just who did the binding here, but it seems most likely that it was *their* father, Ouranos, rather than Kronos. He was the one, after all, who characteristically imprisoned his offspring.

509–620 [502–616] The account of the offspring of the Titans, which has been interrupted by several narrative expansions and suffered a loss of continuity, concludes with the offspring of Iapetos and Klymene: Atlas, Menoitios, Prometheus, and Epimetheus. All were punished by Zeus, and Atlas and Menoitios, at least, seem to have fought alongside their father and uncles against Zeus. This provides the poet with the opportunity to give us a version of the Prometheus story that is a great deal more elaborate than the one in the *Works and Days* (65–125 [45–99]).

525–36 [526–34] There is an apparent contradiction between this passage, in which Zeus is said to have let Herakles kill the eagle and release Prometheus from his "misery," and the end of the Prometheus story below (618 [616]), where Prometheus is still "caught in . . . ineluctable bonds." Either this passage is an interpolation, inconsistent with Hesiod's version of the story, or, as M. L. West suggested *ad loc.*, Hesiod was saying only that Herakles killed the eagle, and so released Prometheus from *that* misery, but left him bound. This is possible, but later versions (including *Prometheus Bound* 710 ff.) present Herakles as the one who will set Prometheus free.

537–62 [535–60] The account of the division of the feast at Mekone, absent from the *Works and Days*, gives us a Prometheus who is more clearly a culture-hero of the trickster type, by whose philanthropic trickery the actual, and advantageous, division of sacrifice was established. There are textual problems here, and this version follows M. L. West's reconstruction. Thus understood, Prometheus' trick was to offer Zeus the (good) meat covered by the (unattractive) paunch, or entrails, leaving the (useless) bones covered by the (rich, attractive) fat for mankind. Zeus said, "This is uneven," to which Prometheus replied, "Take your pick." Zeus picked the (attractive) fat, lifted it up, and found only the bones underneath, and was furious. Hesiod saves Zeus by letting him have it both ways—he saw the trick before he fell for it (553 [551]) but played along with what he saw Prometheus wanted him to do.

563–72 [561–70] The trick provides the motivation for the story of Prometheus the firebringer. Zeus' revenge was taking fire from mankind. They must have had it previously, or the sacrificial feast would have been unthinkable.

573–620 [571–616] Pandora, in turn (who is not named in this version), is the revenge for the theft of fire. Here, there is no pithos (or "box"), and what the nameless woman introduces into the previously all male world of mortals is simply herself: the female. The misogyny is less global but more alarmingly direct. A wife is a lazy drone, a parasite on the labor of her husband. The pessimistic picture recalls the jars of goods and evils on Zeus' doorstep (*Iliad* 24): Just as Zeus can hand out a mix of good and evil, or just pure evil, a good wife will give you a mix in life of good (perhaps, progeny) and bad (by this may be meant the necessity of putting up with even the good wife). The alternative, the abusive wife, brings a life of "incurable evil."

621–67 [617–63] There is no real introduction to the account of the Titanomachy, and (as in the *Iliad*) what is actually narrated is only a small part of the final stage of a war said to have lasted ten years. We do not know exactly in what context Ouranos confined the Hundred-handers (Obriareus, Kottos, and Gyges) underground—perhaps we are to imagine that they were never liberated from their underground prison after Kronos castrated Ouranos, so that they waited deep within their mother for an entire generation before she advised Zeus to liberate them to fight against Kronos and the Titans.

634–43 [630–38] Greek epic narrative does not move freely in time, and tends simply to juxtapose events where we expect more clarification. Here, after being told that the Hundred-handers were liberated to fight on the side of the Olympians, we are given rather abruptly a description of the ten-year stalemate that must have *preceded* that event, before returning to the exchange between Zeus and Kottos, once these powerful allies have been liberated. The eastern portion of the Thessalian plain separates Mt. Olympos from Mt. Othrys.

680–714 [677–710] Note the prevalence of the *sounds* of battle and destruction in this descriptive passage. The crashing and melting and boiling clearly threaten to destroy the order of the universe that we have just seen created.

715–25 [711–23a] The decisive maneuver comes as the Hundred-handers move to the front of the battle lines of the Olympians. In Homeric terms, they become *promachoi*, "fighters in the forefront," who bear the greatest danger and win the greatest glory.

726–825 [724–819] The defeat of the Titans and their confinement in Tartaros provides the context for the poem's description of the underworld and its denizens, among whom it will be no surprise to find a number of the children of Night, catalogued in the opening of the poem. The symmetry of vertical distance, measured by the anvil's fall, implies a remarkably orderly model of the universe, but the important point seems rather to be that the Titans have been put away in a place so remote they are unlikely to pose further problems.

739 [734] The Hundred-handers seem to be put here as the guardians of the Titans, to keep them in their place, but it is odd to find them here

alongside Zeus' defeated enemies, returned to the sort of unpleasant sub-
terranean environment Zeus liberated them from in the first place. Near
the end of the passage (821–25 [815–19]), we hear more about them, and
at that point they are said more appropriately to live in houses set on
the foundations of Ocean (which must be on *this* side of Chaos), and at
least one of them has been rewarded with a Nymph for a wife. The two
descriptions seem mutually contradictory.

751 [750] *the son of Iapetos*: Atlas. It is very difficult to say just *what* he
stands in front of. One possibility is the gates in Poseidon's bronze wall
around the Titans' prison in Tartaros. It is difficult, in any case, to imag-
ine why he would stand in Tartaros to support heaven and earlier (519
[518]) he was performing the same function standing "at Earth's limit"
somewhere near the Hesperides. Clearly, consistency is not essential to
the cosmological poetry.

754–55 [748–50] Tartaros is a bustling city, where deities are sumptuously
housed (just as they are on Olympos). It would seem that Night and Day
share one of those houses, since their needs are eminently compatible.

763–71 [758–66] Night seems to hold Sleep in her arms when she is up in
the world, not while at home in the nether darkness, since Sleep and his
brother Death have their own homes there.

775 [769] *Hound*: Cerberos.

781–812 [775–806] See on 376–405 above. Here, we find out the specific
mechanism by which Styx binds the gods, along with the consequences
for them of their violations of oaths, a process clearly designed to
represent a sort of temporary death, the worst thing that can happen
to an immortal. The verb represented by "loathed" in the translation is
stug*eomai* and constitutes an "etymological" explanation of the name of
the Oceanid and her river. She is what the gods "shudder at," and this is
echoed in the sound of her name.

813–16 [807–10] = 741–44 [736–39] Such repetition is very much charac-
teristic of Greek hexameter poetry, and particularly of Homer, but here
the exact location and nature of these "sources and limits," relative to the
other things beneath the Earth, remains vague. The sense may be simply:
"These are the ends of the universe."

826–85 [820–85] The Typhoios episode is the last challenge to the author-
ity of Zeus—a sort of appendix to the Titanomachy, after the Titans are
already exiled to Tartaros. Gaia (always monstrous) has until this point
seemed sympathetic to Zeus and the Olympians—after all, she came up

with the idea of liberating the Hundred-handers—but for some reason she allies herself with the powers of darkness (Tartaros) and generates one last super-monster. The Titanomachy itself was characterized by outrageous exaggeration and gargantuan scale. This passage goes one step further, testing the limits of the poetic language to describe violence on a cosmic scale.

844 [837] This is perhaps the reason why we need this final assault on Zeus. What is explicitly at stake is sovereignty, and what this poetry of exaggeration does is characteristically to demonize the enemy—the alternative. The conception of the universe as ruled by forces that succeed one another by violent conquest is an upsetting one. Kronos ruled over the Golden Age. His rule was in its day legitimate, and at least susceptible to positive portrayal. The right of Zeus to blast his father's generation into Tartaros is far from obvious. But once it has happened, what is the alternative to the order imposed by Zeus? Typhoios provides an answer: The alternative to Olympian power is something far less tolerable.

875–85 [869–80] Even though he has been blasted into Tartaros, Typhoios' incarnation of violence has its residual effect in the world, in the form of violent and destructive winds.

886–90 [881–85] The suppression of the resistance to the power of Zeus ends with the distribution of honors, rights, and privileges. Gaia's apostasy was apparently only a momentary aberration. She returns here in the role of advisor (and even at Delphi, the official account of the prophetic shrine made her the first to prophesy). With Zeus' distribution (parts of which have been anticipated earlier in the poem), a significant transition occurs, and the last hundred fifty lines of the poem include several new and rather disparate elements.

891–969 [886–962] The genealogical model returns, and we are given the successive matings of Zeus with seven goddesses, two Nymphs, and two mortal women, interspersed with a scattering of matings of Poseidon and of some of the younger Olympians. This completes the population of Olympus, including the Muses and Graces.

891–905 [886–900] Zeus' first wife, Metis (whose name may be translated "cunning intelligence"), reintroduces the theme of the threat of offspring. Earth is again giving the Olympians advice, and along with Ouranos she warns Zeus against the offspring of Metis. Zeus' solution is worthy of his father Kronos; he swallows both the wife and the offspring she contains—at the very least Athena, and perhaps the potential "son," who in any case will never be allowed to pose a threat to the sovereignty of his father. This incorporation of another deity is interesting in that it is also an incorporation of the quality she personifies—by swallowing "cunning intelligence" Zeus appropriates that quality for himself, and in a way that effectively bars all others from access.

906–11 [901–6] Themis ("right") in her reproductive role produces several principles of order in the universe. On the Moirai, see above on 213–34.

929–34 [921–29] That Athena was born from the head of Zeus was a very widespread story, but that Metis, whom Zeus swallowed many marriages back (see on 891–905, above), was in some sense her mother, is peculiar to the Hesiodic account. Likewise, Homer has Hephaistos treat Zeus as his father, so he is presumably innocent of the idea that Hera produced him parthenogenetically in retaliation for Zeus' giving birth to Athena.

939–43 [933–37] Another development that conflicts with the Homeric treatment of these deities: In Homer, Aphrodite (the daughter of Zeus) was Ares' sister and adulterous lover (*Odyssey* 8, "The Song of Ares and Aphrodite"), and her legitimate husband was Hephaistos, who got revenge for his cuckoldry. The liaison lent itself to rich allegorical readings: What Homer was really representing was the complementary nature of love and strife, which constitute the dynamics of the universe, and so forth. Hesiod's version looks very much as if it started from that sort of reading of Ares and Aphrodite, since all their offspring are personifications, giving anthropomorphic divine form to "Rout" and "Terror" as well as "Harmony."

949 [942] *They are both divine now*: Euripides' *Bacchae* is usually taken as the standard version of this story, and there, Semele has clearly been divinized by the apparition of Zeus the lightning god that consumed her. Dionysos was then sewn in Zeus' thigh to be born a second time.

954–56 [947–49] After Ariadne helped Theseus, he abandoned her on Naxos, where Dionysos found her and took her to Olympos.

964–69 [956–62] The account of the generations of the gods ends with a series of liminal figures, violators of the barrier between divinity and mortality (Dionysos, Herakles, Ariadne), and finally, the children of the Sun (Helios): Kirke, who was a Nymph like her mother, and Aiëtes, who was presumably mortal, but got a Nymph for a wife and produced Medeia, one of the most richly ambiguous figures in Greek myth. (See on 1000–1010 [992–1002], below.)

970–1030 [963–1020] The last fifty lines of the poem turn explicitly to a new subject: "the goddesses who slept with mortal men." This fifty-line poem was in turn balanced by the Hesiodic *Catalogue of Women* (which survives only in the form of a very rich collection of fragments), the core of which is the mortal women who slept with gods (see on 1029–30 [1021–22], below).

1000–1010 [992–1002] Here, in the lists of goddesses who slept with men, we find Medeia's story—a less familiar variant, in which she has only one child, named after herself (Medeios).

1016–18 [1008–10] Most Greek aristocratic families probably traced their pedigrees to women who had borne children to gods (cf. below on the *Catalogue of Women*), but of course the most egregious use of this archaic poetry to legitimate political power turns on this story: the divine birth of Aineias (Aeneas), whom the Julio-Claudian emperors of Rome claimed as the founder of their line.

1019–26 [1011–20] The last affairs of immortal women with mortal men in Hesiod's list are the loves of Odysseus, familiar from the *Odyssey*. Some of the stories of these (non-Homeric) offspring of Odysseus by Circe and Kalypso were told in the lost epic called the *Telegoneia*, which followed the *Odyssey* in the sequence of the Epic Cycle. This poetry that legitimates power is of course highly subject to manipulation, and it is somewhat distressing to find Latinus, the lord of the Etruscans (Tyrsenians) given an Odyssean pedigree here, in close juxtaposition with the story of the birth of Aineias. Neither Latinus nor the Etruscans are mentioned in Greek again until the classical period.

1029–30 [1021–22] The closing lines form a bridge to the lost *Catalogue of Women*. Thus, in a sense, our *Theogony* is a prologue to that catalogue, which in turn may well represent the oldest and in a sense the most important of the early Greek epic poetry known to us. "Important," that is, in its original context, because epic poetry presents itself as having the primary function of perpetuating the praise of the heroes of the past, but of more practical importance for the Greeks of the archaic and classical periods, this poetry legitimated their status by singing the praise of their ancestors (actual or claimed). The *Catalogue* was therefore of tremendous importance, since aristocratic pedigrees normally began with a god, and so this poem was in fact a catalogue of the stories of the origins of most of the aristocratic bloodlines (see on 1016–18 [1008–10], above).

GLOSSARY

This selective list of some of the major figures and geographical names in the poems of Hesiod is limited for the most part to names that occur more than once in the two poems. For major figures in mythology, some additional, non-Hesiodic information is supplied, but a mythological dictionary must be consulted for a more complete account of all the figures in the poem.

Abyss see Chaos
  Th 116; 704

Aegisholder
Epithet of Zeus. However, the *aigis* (goatskin) was used as a shield by Athene, not Zeus, and the regular application of this Homeric and Hesiodic epithet to Zeus is problematic.
  Th 12; 14; 26; 925; 973; 1030

Aether ("bright sky")
Child of Night and Erebos. The common noun designates the dry, fiery part of the gaseous envelope of the Earth, in contrast to *aer* ("mist," "air") which is moist.
  Th 125

Agaue
1. Nereid Nymph.
  Th 248
2. Daughter of Kadmos and Harmonia; wife of Ekhion; sister of Ino, Semele, Autonoe and Polydoros; mother of Pentheus.
  Th 984

Aglaia
One of the Graces. Wife of Hephaistos.
  Th 914; 953

Aiakos
Traditionally, one of the judges of the underworld.
  Th 1012

Aietes
King of Kolkhis. Son of Helios and Perseis; husband of Idyia; father of Medeia.
  Th 964; 965; 1000; 1001

Aigaion, Mount
Aigaion is the name given by Hesiod to the mountain in Crete where Zeus was born. It cannot be located with any certainty, since it is impossible to be certain which of the Zeus-caves of Crete is referred to here.
   Th 487

Aineias
Hero of Troy. Son of Ankhises and Aphrodite. Later tradition made him the ancestor of the founders of Rome.
   Th 1016

Akhaians
Properly, the people of Akhaia, but in Homeric and Hesiodic usage, the Greeks in general.
   W 722

Akhilles
Son of Peleus and Thetis; the principal Akhaian hero during the siege of Troy.
   Th 1015

Alkmene
Wife of Amphitryon; mother of twin sons: Herakles (by Zeus) and Iphikles (by Amphitryon).
   Th 529; 950; 957

Amphitrite
Nereid Nymph; wife of Poseidon; mother of Triton.
   Th 244; 254; 935

Amphitryon
Husband of Alkmene; father of Iphikles, twin half-brother of Herakles, who was fathered by Zeus, who seduced Alkmene by appearing as Amphitryon.
   Th 317

Ankhises
An elder of Troy. Father of Aineias, by Aphrodite.
   Th 1017

Apesas
Mountain near Nemea.
   Th 332

Aphrodite
One of the twelve deities of Olympos; in Hesiod, born from the severed genitals of Ouranos, and associated primarily with sexual passion.
   Th 17; 828; 939; 982; 988; 997; 1013; 1022
   W 84; 582

Apollo
One of the twelve deities of Olympos. Son of Zeus and Leto; twin brother of Artemis. God of light, plague and healing, music, archery, and prophecy, especially at Delphoi.
  Th 15; 96; 349; 923
  W 852

Arcturus
A bright star in the constellation Boötes, important for Hesiodic astronomy.
  W 628; 675

Ares (= War)
One of the twelve deities of Olympos. Only son of Zeus and Hera; father (by Aphrodite) of Harmonia and of Phobos and Deimos.
  Th 927; 939; 941

Argos
Major city in the northeast Peloponnesos. The Argive Heraion was one of Hera's most important shrines.
  Th 13

Ariadne
Daughter of Minos and Pasiphae; abandoned by Theseus, she became the wife of Dionysos.
  Th 954

Arima
Apparently the name of a mountain range in which the monster-nymph Echidna lurks, eating raw meat, but the toponym is obscure.
  Th 305

Artemis
One of the twelve deities of Olympos. Virgin daughter of Zeus and Leto; twin sister of Apollo. Artemis is the patroness of fertility and childbirth, wildlife and hunting.
  Th 15; 923

Askra
Town in the Valley of the Muses, below Mt. Helikon. Hesiod claims it as his home.
  W 707

Asteria
Daughter of Koios and Phoibe; sister of Leto; mother (by Perses) of Hekate.
  Th 411

Astraios ("starry")
Son of Krios and Eurybia; brother of Pallas and Perses; husband of Eos; father of Zephyros, Boreas, Notos, and Dawnstar (Heosphoros).
Th 377; 379

Athene
One of the twelve deities of Olympos. Virgin daughter of Zeus and Metis. Zeus swallowed the pregnant Metis, fearing that she would give birth to a child more powerful than himself, and some time later gave birth to Athene through his head. Athene was venerated as the goddess of wisdom and war, patroness of civic responsibilities, arts, and crafts.
Th 14; 329; 575; 579; 894; 929
W 83; 91; 96; 483

Atlas
Son of Iapetos and Klymene; brother of Epimetheus, Prometheus, and Menoitios; father of the Pleiades. Zeus condemned him to hold up the sky, apparently to punish him for siding with the Titans.
Th 511; 519

Aulis
A town in Boeotia. The Akhaian fleet assembled there to sail against Troy; Hesiod once set sail from there on his way to Euboia.
W 722

Autonoe
1. Nereid Nymph.
    Th 259
2. Daughter of Kadmos and Harmonia; mother of Aktaion.
    Th 984

Avengers see Furies
Th 477

Bellerophon
Corinthian hero. Son of Glaukos and Eurymede. The winged horse Pegasos accompanied him on his exploits.
Th 326

Boreas (= North Wind)
Son of Astraios and Eos; brother of Notos, Zephyros, and Dawnstar (Heosphoros).
Th 380; 876
W 567; 574; 608; 614

Briareos (= Obriareos)
One of the Hundred-handers. Son of Ouranos and Gaia.
Th 150; 622; 739; 823

Cerberos
Hades' multiheaded dog, who guarded the entrance to the underworld, offspring of Typhaon/Typhoios and Echidna. As one of his labors, Herakles dragged Cerberos up to show him to Eurystheus of Tiryns, and then dragged him back down to the underworld.
Th 312

Chaos (= Abyss)
The Greek word *khaos* is related to the verb "gape" and refers properly to a "gaping" or opening up of a hole or chasm.
Th 116, Chaos the Abyss; Abyss 123; 704; 820

Chimaira
A fire-breathing monster with the head of a lion, the body of a goat, and a serpent's tail; offspring of Typhaon/Typhoios and Echidna. Bellerophon flew in on Pegasos and killed her.
Th 320

Chiron
A centaur, tutor of Akhilles, but mentioned in Hesiod only as the tutor of Jason and Medeia's son Medeios.
Th 1009

Chrysaor ("golden sword")
Son of Poseidon and Medousa; brother of Pegasos; husband of Kallirhoe; father of Geryones and Echidna. Chrysaor was born holding a golden sword in his hand, emerging from the beheaded body of Medousa after Perseus killed her.
Th 282; 284; 288; 988

Crete
The largest Greek island, marking the southern limit of the Aegean Sea. Birthplace of Zeus in Hesiod's account.
Th 481; 484; 978

Cyclopes (singular: Cyclops)
Sons of Ouranos and Gaia. Hesiod names three of them: Brontes, Steropes, and Arges. Forgers of Zeus' thunderbolts, they were called Cyclopes ("round-eyes") because each of them had only one large eye in the middle of his forehead.
Th 140; 145

Dawn see Eos
  Th 373; 379; 454; 992
  W 675

Dawnstar see Heosphoros
  Th 382

Deimos ("terror")
Son of Ares and Aphrodite; brother of Phobos and Harmonia.
  Th 940

Demeter
One of the twelve deities of Olympos. Daughter of Kronos and Rheia; sister of Zeus; mother of Persephone (by Zeus) and of Ploutos (by Iasion). Demeter was venerated as the patroness of agriculture, with her principal shrine at Eleusis.
  Th 458; 917; 976
  W 43; 343; 441; 522; 523; 662; 903

Destinies see Ker(es)
  Th 217

Dike (= Justice)
Daughter of Zeus and Themis. Dike is the personification of justice (or simply of "doing right" as opposed to criminal behavior).
  Th 907
  W 253; Justice, 255; 296; 325

Dione
In Hesiod, an Oceanid Nymph (*Th.* 357 [353]). According to Homer, Dione was the mother (by Zeus) of Aphrodite; Hesiod relates a different myth concerning Aphrodite's birth, but her position of honor in the hymn of the Muses (*Th.* 18 [17]) suggests some acknowledgment of her high status.
  Th 18; 355

Dionysos
One of the twelve deities of Olympos. Son of Zeus and Semele; husband of Ariadne. Dionysos was associated with wine and ecstatic initiatory ritual.
  Th 948; 954
  W 680

Doris
1. Oceanid Nymph, wife of Nereus; mother of the Nereids.
  Th 240; 352

2. Nereid Nymph (named for her mother).
   Th 251

Earth see Gaia
   Th 46; 107; 117; 126; 160; 174; 178; 184; 231; 237; 424; 467; 474; 483;
   497; 507; 630; 649; 707; 708; 741; 813; 827; 846; 854; 865; 896
   W 625

Echidna ("viper")
Underworld deity. Daughter of Chrysaor and Kallirhoe. She was half
serpent and half Nymph, and mother of a brood of monsters.
   Th 298; 305

Eileithyia
Daughter of Zeus and Hera; sister of Ares and Hebe. Venerated as the
goddess of childbirth.
   Th 927

Eirene ("peace")
Daughter of Zeus and Themis.
   Th 907

Elektra
Oceanid Nymph; wife of Thaumas; mother of Iris and of the Harpies.
   Th 267; 351

Eleutherae
Town on the border between Attica and Boeotia.
   Th 54

Envy see Zeal
   W 227

Eos (= Dawn)
Daughter of Hyperion and Theia; sister of Helios and Selene; wife
of Astraios; mother of Zephyros, Boreas, Notos and Heosphoros
(Dawnstar).
   Th 20; 373; Dawn, 454; 992
   W 675 (Dawn)

Epimetheus ("hindsight")
A Titan. Son of Iapetos and Klymene; brother of Prometheus, Menoitios
and Atlas. He accepted the first mortal woman, Pandora, as a gift from
the gods.
   Th 513
   W 103; 105; 109

Erebos
One of the primeval deities. Father (by his sister Night) of Aether and Day.
   Th 123; 125; 517; Underworld, 673

Eris (= Strife)
Daughter of Night; see n. on *W&D* 21.
   Th 225; 226
   W 21; strife, 22; 28; 37; strife, 43; 901

Eros (= Desire)
One of Hesiod's primeval deities.
   Th 201

Erytheia
An island in the river Okeanos, beyond the Pillars of Herakles. The island
was the home of Geryones, whose cattle Herakles was sent to bring back
to Tiryns as one of his labors.
   Th 291; 991

Euboia
An island off the coast of Attike and Boeotia. Hesiod mentions it as the
only place to which he ever sailed on the open sea.
   W 722

Eunomia ("good laws")
Daughter of Zeus and Themis.
   Th 907

Eurybia
Daughter of Pontos and Gaia; wife of Krios; mother of Astraios, Pallas,
and Perses.
   Th 239; 376

Eurynome
Oceanid Nymph; third wife of Zeus and mother of the Graces.
   Th 360; 912

Eurytion
Geryon's herdsman, killed by Herakles when he stole the cattle.
   Th 294

Fate, Fates see Moirai
   Th 211; 218
   W 113

Furies (= Avengers)
According to Hesiod, the Furies are daughters of Gaia, conceived when
she was spattered with blood from the severed genitals of Ouranos.

Th 185; avengers, 477
W 900

Gaia (= Earth)
One of the primeval deities who came into existence out of Chaos. Mother and wife of Ouranos; mother of many of the first generation of gods.
Th 21; 117; 148; 154; 850; 888
W 625 (earth)

Geryon (or Geryones)
A three-headed (or three-bodied) Giant. Son of Chrysaor and Kallirhoe. The theft of his cattle was one of the labors of Herakles.
Th 288; 310; 990

Giants
Huge, monstrous beings who came into existence when blood from the severed genitals of Ouranos was spattered on Gaia.
Th 50; 186

Gorgons
Three sisters usually represented as monstrous: Stheno, Euryale, and Medousa. Daughters of Phorkys and Keto; sisters of the Graiai. Only Medousa was mortal, and she was killed by Perseus.
Th 275

Graces
Daughters of Zeus and Eurynome: Aglaia, Euphrosyne, and Thalia. The Graces often accompany the Muses.
Th 65; 913; 953
W 92

Graiai ("old women")
Three sisters: Pemphredo, Enyo, and Deino (Hesiod names only the first two). Daughters of Phorkys and Keto; sisters of the Gorgons, gray-haired from birth.
Th 271; 273

Gyges
One of the Hundred-handers. Son of Ouranos and Gaia.
Th 150; 623; 717; 739; 823

Hades
Lord of the underworld; ruler of the dead. Son of Kronos and Rheia; brother of Zeus and Poseidon; husband of Persephone.
Th 312; 459; 773; 780; 857; 918
W 175

Harmonia
Daughter of Ares and Aphrodite; wife of Kadmos; mother of Ino, Semele, Agaue, Autonoe, and Polydoros.
   Th 942; 982

Harpies ("snatchers")
Daughters of Thaumas and Elektra. Hesiod says only that they flew with the winds, but various myths depict them snatching up and carrying off things and people. He names only Aello and Ocypete, but other sources add a third, Celaeno.
   Th 268

Heaven see Ouranos
   Th 126; 159; 424; 467; 474; 649; 706; 847; 896

Hebe
Daughter of Zeus and Hera; wife of Herakles after his death and installation in Olympos, where she served as cupbearer to the gods. Her name means "youth."
   Th 18; 917; 959

Hekate
Daughter of Perses and Asteria. After the defeat of the Titans, Zeus allowed her to retain her powers, and she was venerated as one who bestows good fortune on mortals. Hekate was often worshipped at crossroads.
   Th 413; 420; 443; 455

Helen
Wife of King Menelaos of Sparta. The Trojan Paris abducted her to Troy, provoking the ten-year siege of that city in the attempt to retrieve her.
   W 187

Helikon, Mount
The largest mountain in Boeotia, sacred to the Muses. Hesiod claims to be a native of Askra, a village on the slopes of Mt. Helikon, where he says he first encountered the Muses while he was tending sheep.
   Th 2; 7; 24
   W 706

Helios ("sun")
Son of Hyperion and Theia; brother of Selene and Eos; husband of Klymene; father (by Perseis) of Aietes, Kirke, and Phaethon.
   Th 20; 372; 764; 963; 965; 1019

Hellas = Greece
  W 724

Hephaistos
One of the twelve deities of Olympos. Son of Zeus and Hera (or of Hera alone); brother of Ares, Hebe, and Eileithyia. The lame smith god, he was venerated as the patron deity of the forge, of volcanoes and fire, and of arts and crafts which require fire for their practice.
  Th 872; 933; 952
  W 78

Hera
One of the twelve deities of Olympos. Daughter of Kronos and Rheia; sister and wife of Zeus; mother of Hephaistos, Ares, Hebe, and Eileithyia. Hera was venerated as the patroness of women and marriage.
  Th 12; 316; 330; 458; 926; 932; 960

Herakles
Best known of the Heroes. Son of Zeus and Alkmene; half-brother of his twin Iphikles, who was fathered by Amphitryon. Several of his labors are recounted in capsule form in the *Theogony*, usually in the context of explaining the genealogy of the monsters he killed. After his death and admission to Olympos, he married Hebe.
  Th 290; 316; 333; 529; 532; 950; 957; 990

Hermes
One of the twelve deities of Olympos. Son of Zeus and Maia. Hermes is the herald and messenger of the gods, the patron of roads and travelers, of theft and deceit, athletics, animal fertility, and communications. He was responsible for escorting the souls of the dead to the underworld.
  Th 446; 945
  W 86; 104

Hesperides
Daughters of Night. They lived on an island in the river Okeanos, beyond the Pillars of Herakles, far in the west, where they guarded the tree which produced the famous golden apples.
  Th 215; 276

Hestia
Virgin daughter of Kronos and Rheia; sister of Zeus. Hestia was the patron deity of the hearth and the protector of home and family. She was worshipped at the fireside in every home, and every city had a public hearth, from whose perpetual fire a lighted torch was brought to new colonies.
  Th 458

Hyades
Seven stars in the constellation Taurus. When they rise with the sun, they are an indication that the rainy season has come.
  W 681

Hydra
A monstrous water serpent. Offspring of Typhaon/Typhoios and Echidna. Herakles killed the Hydra as one of his labors.
  Th 314; 315

Hyperion
A Titan. Son of Ouranos and Gaia; husband of Theia; father of Helios, Selene, and Eos.
  Th 134; 375; 1019

Iapetos
A Titan. Son of Ouranos and Gaia; husband of Klymene; father of Prometheus, Epimetheus, Menoitios, and Atlas.
  Th 19; 509; 530; 545; 561; 567; 618; 751
  W 72; 761

Ida, Mount
A mountain near Troy in northwest Asia Minor.
  Th 1018

Idyia
Oceanid Nymph; wife of Aietes; mother of Medeia.
  Th 354

Ino
Daughter of Kadmos and Harmonia; sister of Agaue, Autonoe, Semele, and Polydoros; wife of Athamas. As the goddess Leucothoe, she saved the shipwrecked Odysseus.
  Th 983

Iolaos
Companion and charioteer of his uncle Herakles.
  Th 319

Iris
Daughter of Thaumas and Elektra; sister of the Harpies. Iris served as a messenger for the gods.
  Th 267; 786; 790

Jason
A Hero, leader of the Argonauts. Son of Aison; husband of Medeia; father of Medeios.
  Th 1008

Justice see Dike
  W 253; 255; 296; 325

Kadmos
Founder and king of Thebes in Boeotia. Son of Agenor; brother of Europa; husband of Harmonia; father of Agaue, Autonoe, Ino, Semele, and Polydoros.
  Th 943; 983
  W 184

Kallirhoe
Oceanid Nymph; wife of Chrysaor; mother of Geryon and, according to Hesiod, of Echidna.
  Th 289; 987

Kalypso
Oceanid Nymph; lover of Odysseus; mother of Nausinoos and Nausithoos.
  Th 361; 1025

Keto ("Sea monster," "whale")
Daughter of Pontos and Gaia; wife of Phorkys; mother of the Graiai and the Gorgons.
  Th 238

Khalkis
City in Euboia visited by Hesiod.
  W 725

Kirke
Daughter of Helios and Perseis; sister of Aietes. Kirke was the sorceress who turned Odysseus' crew into swine.
  Th 964; 1019

Klymene
Oceanid Nymph; wife of the Titan Iapetos; mother of Prometheus, Epimetheus, Menoitios, and Atlas.
  Th 353; 510

Koios
A Titan. Son of Ouranos and Gaia; husband of Phoibe; father of Leto and Asteria.
  Th 406

Kottos
One of the Hundred-handers. Son of Ouranos and Gaia.
  Th 134

Krios
A Titan. Son of Ouranos and Gaia; husband of Eurybia; father of Astraios, Pallas, and Perses.
  Th 134

Kronion (dim. of Kronos)
Patronymic of Zeus.
  Th 4; 53; 536; 956

Kronos
A Titan, last born but most important. Son of Ouranos and Gaia; husband of his sister Rheia; father of Zeus and other deities.
  Th 19; 74; 138; 169; 175; 397; 413; 425; 452; 456; 463; 470; 476; 480; 489; 497; 629; 630; 636; 639; 651; 664; 672; 858
  W 30; 89; 131; 160; 195; 280; 299; 318

Kyme
Aiolian city on the west coast of Asia Minor, roughly midway between Smyrna and Pergamon. Hesiod tells us that his father came from there.
  W 703

Kypros (= Cyprus)
Eastern Mediterranean island near the south coast of Asia Minor, sacred to Aphrodite.
  Th 193; 199

Kythera
An island south of the Peloponnese, sacred to Aphrodite.
  Th 198

Kythereia (= Aphrodite)
Epithet of Aphrodite, associated by Hesiod with Kythera.
  Th 197; 1016

Leto
Daughter of Koios and Phoibe; mother (by Zeus) of Apollo and Artemis.
  Th 19; 408; 923
  W 851

Lord of Lightning
Epithet of Zeus.
  Th 392

Lyktos
A city in east central Crete, near which Hesiod locates the birthplace of Zeus.
  Th 481; 485

Maia
Atlantid Nymph; mother (by Zeus) of Hermes.
  Th 944

Medeia
Daughter of Aietes and Idyia; wife of Jason, whom she helped to steal the Golden Fleece. She was a sorceress like her aunt Kirke.
  Th 968

Medousa
One of the Gorgons. Poseidon impregnated her before Perseus killed her, and Chrysaor and Pegasos emerged from her decapitated body. The motif of her ugliness turning viewers to stone is not Hesiodic. Snake-haired and boar-toothed, the face of Medousa was reproduced in many places as an apotropaic talisman.
  Th 277

Mekone
Identified as Sikyon, west of Corinth, where Prometheus sacrificed an ox to the gods and tricked Zeus into accepting only the bones and fat, leaving the better, edible parts for mortals.
  Th 538

Meliai
Ash-tree Nymphs.
  Th 187

Memnon
King of Ethiopia. Son of Tithonos and Eos.
  Th 992

Memory see Mnemosyne
  Th 54

Menoitios
Son of Iapetos and Klymene; brother of Prometheus, Epimetheus, and Atlas. Zeus banished him to Erebos after the Titanomachy.
  Th 512; 516

Metis ("cunning intelligence")
Oceanid Nymph; first wife of Zeus; mother of Athene. While she was pregnant, Zeus swallowed Metis; Athene was later born from his head.
  Th 360; 891; 899

Minos
King of Crete. Son of Zeus and Europa. Eventually, one of the judges in the underworld.
  Th 955

Mnemosyne (= Memory)
A Titan. Daughter of Ouranos and Gaia; mother (by Zeus) of the Muses.
   Th 54, memory; 135; 920

Moirai (= Fates)
Daughters of Night: Hesiod gives them the names Klotho, Lakhesis, and Atropos. They are difficult to distinguish in function from the Keres (= Destinies).
   Th 217, destinies; 910

Muses
Divine patronesses of the arts, nine daughters of Zeus and Mnemosyne.
   Th 1; 26; 35; 37; 52; 76; 96; 98; 101; 114; 921; 972; 1029
   W 1; 729; 733

Nemea
Site of the Nemean Games, south of Corinth, once ravaged by a lion sent by Hera. The lion was the offspring of Orthos and Chimaira (or possibly Echidna). As one of his labors, Herakles killed the lion and afterwards habitually clothed himself in its skin.
   Th 330

Nemesis ("retribution," "indignation")
Daughter of Night. Personification of retribution, or rather of the proper response to wrongdoing. Coupled by Homer and Hesiod with Shame (*aidos*).
   Th 223

Nereid Nymphs
The daughters of Nereus and Doris, of whom Hesiod names about fifty (*Th.* 246–65 [243–62]).
   Th 244

Nereus
Sea deity. Son of Pontos; husband of Doris; father of many of the sea, river, and water deities.
   Th 233; 240; 264; 1011

Night
One of the primeval deities. She is the mother of many of the first generation of gods who personify some of the less pleasant aspects of life.
   Th 21; 108; 123; 124; 177; 211; 213; 223; 731; 749; 753; 762; 763
   W 29

North Wind see Boreas
   W 608; 614

Notos (= South Wind)
Son of Astraios and Eos; brother of Zephyros, Boreas and Dawnstar (Heosphoros).
Th 381; 876
W 749

Nymphs
Female deities associated with various features of the natural landscape such as springs, rivers, forests, mountains, etc. See Oceanid Nymphs, Nereid Nymphs.
Th 130; 187

Obriareos see Briareos
Th 622

Ocean See Okeanos
Th 133; 216; 241; 266; 275; 283; 289; 293; 295; 339; 364; 366; 369; 384; 390; 509; 698; 782; 795; 797; 822; 848; 912; 967; 987
W 192; 628

Oceanid Nymphs
The three thousand daughters of Ocean and Tethys, forty-one of whom are named by Hesiod (*Th*. 353–65 [349–61]).
Th 351

Odysseus
Hero of the *Odyssey*. Son of Laertes and Antikleia; husband of Penelope; King of Ithaca.
Th 1020; 1025

Oidipous
King of Thebes. Hesiod mentions him only as the owner of the cattle whose acquisition cost the lives of several Heroes.
W 185

Okeanos (= Ocean)
A Titan. Son of Ouranos and Gaia; brother and husband of Tethys; father of numerous water deities. Rather than meaning "ocean" in the modern sense, Okeanos personified the great river which was thought to flow all around the dry land of earth and to which all other rivers were connected.
Th 21; 361; 369; 987
W 192, ocean; 628, ocean

Olympian
As principal deity of Olympos, Zeus is called "*the* Olympian."
Th 889
W 101; 107; 148; 283; 297

Olympos
Highest mountain in Greece, considered the home of the twelve principal gods.
   Th 38; 51; 63; 69; 76; 102; 113; 393; 399; 410; 531; 638; 683; 693; 789; 799; 810; 849; 862; 959
   W 130; 230

Orion
Conspicuous constellation, prominent in Hesiodic astronomy. Before he became a constellation, a giant famed as a hunter.
   W 661; 674; 681; 685

Orthos
Monstrous dog. Offspring of Typhaon/Typhoios and Echidna. He subsequently fathered several other monsters. Orthos belonged to Geryon, who used him to guard his cattle. Herakles killed Orthos when he took the cattle.
   Th 294; 310; 328

Ouranians
Patronymic clan name for the Titans in general, or for deities who were half-Titan.
   Th 465; 924; 934

Ouranos (= Sky, Heaven)
The first dominant male deity in Hesiod's cosmogony, son and consort of Gaia; father of many of her children, the Titans.
   Th 148; 177; 207; 503

Pallas
1. Son of Krios and Eurybia; brother of Astraios and Perses; husband of Styx; father of Vying, Victory, Strength, and Force.
   Th 377
2. Epithet of Athene, probably in connection with her role as a war goddess.
   Th 579
   W 96

Pandora
The first mortal woman, crafted of clay by Hephaistos and adorned by the other gods of Olympos and the Graces in an attempt to trick Prometheus into accepting her—along with her jarful of miseries—as a gift from Zeus.
   W 101

Parnassos, Mount
Mt. Parnassos is a huge massif north of the Gulf of Corinth in central Greece. Delphoi, sacred to Apollo, is located on its south slopes.
Th 502

Pegasos
The winged horse who emerged from the beheaded body of Medousa. Son of Poseidon and Medousa; brother of Chrysaor; companion and helper of Bellerophon.
Th 282; 285; 326

Peitho (= Persuasion)
Oceanid Nymph. Peitho helped adorn Pandora.
Th 351
W 93 Persuasion

Peleus
King of Phthia. Father (by Thetis) of Akhilles.
Th 1014

Pelias
King of Iolkos. Pelias usurped the throne of the rightful king, his brother Aison. It was Pelias who sent his nephew Jason after the Golden Fleece.
Th 1004

Perseis
Oceanid Nymph; mother (by Helios) of Aietes and Kirke.
Th 358; 964

Persephone
Daughter of Zeus and Demeter; wife of Hades, who abducted her and brought her to the underworld.
Th 773; 918

Perses
1. In the *Works and Days*, brother of the poet Hesiod and addressee of the poem.
W 19; 42; 246; 316; 329; 341; 360; 402; 447; 676; 699; 711
2. In the *Theogony*, son of the Titan Krios; father of Hekate.
Th 378; 411

Perseus
A Hero. Son of Zeus and Danae. Perseus beheaded Medousa in one of his exploits.
Th 281

Persuasion see Peitho
 W 93

Phobos ("rout" in Homeric Greek, later and in nonmilitary contexts, "fear")
Son of Ares and Aphrodite; brother of Deimos and Harmonia.
 Th 940

Phoibe
A Titan. Daughter of Ouranos and Gaia; wife of Koios; mother of Leto and Asteria.
 Th 406

Phoibos ("radiant")
Epithet of Apollo.
 Th 15

Phorkys
Sea deity. Son of Pontos and Gaia; brother of Thaumas, Keto, and Eurybia; husband of his sister Keto; father of the Gorgons and the Graiai and (by Hekate) of Skylla.
 Th 238; 271; 334; 338

Pieria
Mountainous region north of Mt. Olympos, sacred to the Muses.
 Th 53
 W 1

Ploutos ("wealth")
Agricultural deity. Son of Iasion and Demeter.
 Th 976

Pontos (= Sea)
Unfathered son of Gaia; father of Nereus. By Gaia, he fathered Thaumas, Phorkys, Keto, and Eurybia.
 Th 233

Poseidon
One of the twelve deities of Olympos. Son of Kronos and Rheia; brother of Zeus and Hades; father (by Amphitrite) of Triton. Poseidon was the patron of horses and god of earthquakes and the sea.
 Th 460; 737; 824
 W 738

Prometheus ("Foresight")
Son of Iapetos and Klymene; brother of Epimetheus, Atlas, and Menoitios. A trickster whose story occurs in slightly different forms in either

poem; credited with the gift of fire to mankind and the establishment of the norms of sacrifice.

Th 512; 523; 536; 538; 548; 618

W 66; 106

Psamathe

Nereid Nymph, wife of Aiakos; mother of Phokos.

Th 261; 1012

Quicksilver (= Hermes)

W 86; 97; 104 Hermes

Rheia

A Titan. Daughter of Ouranos and Gaia; sister and wife of Kronos; mother of Zeus, Hera, Demeter, Poseidon, and other deities.

Th 135; 456; 472

Rivers

Sons of Okeanos and Tethys. Hesiod names twenty-five of them (*Th.* 342–49 [338–45]).

Th 349

Sea see Pontos

Th 108; 131; 233; 237

Seasons

Daughters of Zeus and Themis. The Seasons helped adorn Pandora and were venerated as patronesses of life and growth.

Th 906

W 94

Selene ("moon")

Daughter of Hyperion and Theia; sister of Helios and Eos.

Th 20; 372

Semele

Daughter of Kadmos and Harmonia; mother (by Zeus) of Dionysos. Hera, jealous of Semele's relationship with Zeus, tricked her into asking him to reveal himself in all the splendor of his divinity. His ensuing apparition in a firestorm of thunder and lightning promptly incinerated poor Semele, but Zeus took the unborn Dionysos from her ashes and placed him inside his thigh until it was time for him to be born.

Th 946; 983

Sirius

The brightest star in the constellation known as Canis Major ("Orion's Dog"), the Dog Star.

W 469; 649; 674

Sky see Ouranos
  Th 46; 107

Sphinx
A lioness with a human head, she was called 'Phix' in Boeotia; she installed herself on Mt. Phikion, just west of Thebes, where she accosted travelers.
  Th 327

Storm King see Zeus
  Th 52; 740
  W 543; 732

Strife see Eris
  W 21; 37

Styx
Oceanid Nymph; wife of Pallas; mother of Vying, Victory, Strength, and Force. Styx and her children were the first to come to Olympos in response to Zeus' request for help in his battle against the Titans. The children remain with Zeus, but she lives by the river in the underworld that has her name; she serves as the gods' oath.
  Th 363; 384; 390; 399; 782; 812

Tartaros
Region beyond Chaos where the Titans were imprisoned.
  Th 119; 685; 725; 730; 741; 813; 828; 848; 858; 874

Tethys
A Titan. Daughter of Ouranos and Gaia; wife of Okeanos; mother of numerous Rivers and Nymphs.
  Th 136; 339; 364; 369

Thaumas
Son of Pontos and Gaia; husband of Elektra; father of Iris and the Harpies.
  Th 237; 266; 786

Thebes
Principal city of Boeotia.
  Th 986
  W 184

Theia
A Titan. Daughter of Ouranos and Gaia; wife of Hyperion; mother of Helios, Selene, and Eos.
  Th 135; 372; 375

Themis
A Titan. Daughter of Ouranos and Gaia; wife of Zeus; mother of Euno-
mia, Dike, Eirene, the Moirai, and the Seasons. Her name means "right,"
and as her offspring suggest, she was conceived as the source of many of
the important ordering principles of the universe.
   Th 17; 135; 906

Thetis
Nereid Nymph; wife of Peleus; mother of Akhilles.
   Th 245; 1014

Thrace
The region between Macedonia and the Black Sea, and, from a Greek
perspective, the cold north.
   W 568

Tiryns
City near Argos from which Herakles set out upon his labors at the
command of Eurystheus.
   Th 293

Titans
Children of Ouranos and Gaia. The Titans were the first generation of
gods, later coming into conflict with Zeus and the other new gods of Olym-
pos. Hesiod identifies six male and six female Titans in the original group:
Okeanos, Koios, Krios, Hyperion, Iapetos, and Kronos; Theia, Rheia, The-
mis, Mnemosyne, Phoibe, and Tethys. See n. at *Theogony* 209–12.
   Th 394; 426; 636; 637; 651; 653; 667; 672; 677; 679; 700; 721; 734; 820;
   826; 858; 888

Tretos
Mountain southeast of Nemea, where the lion's den was located.
   Th 332

Triton
Sea deity. Son of Poseidon and Amphitrite. Triton sounds trumpet blasts
on a conch shell.
   Th 936

Troy
In the *Iliad*, city in northwest Asia Minor besieged by the Akhaians in
their attempt to retrieve Helen.
   W 187; 724 (twice)

Typhaon (= Typhoios)
   Th 308

Typhoios
A hundred-headed giant. Son of Tartaros and Gaia. Zeus buried him
among the Arimoi, where he mated with Echidna, fathering a brood of
monsters.
  Th 829; 844; 875

Tyrsenians ("Etruscans")
A nation of central Italy. The Romans called them "Etrusci."
  Th 1024

West Wind see Zephyros
  W 657

Zephyros (= West Wind)
Son of Astraios and Eos; brother of Boreas, Notos, and Dawnstar
(Heosphoros).
  Th 380; 876
  W 657 West Wind

Zeus (= Kronion, Storm King)
Ruler of the twelve deities of Olympos. Son of Kronos and Rheia.
  Th 12; 26; 30; 37; 42; 48; 51; 56; 77; 82; 97; 105; 142; 287; 317; 329;
  350; 389; 401; 413; 430; 461; 469; 473; 483; 501; 516; 522; 531; 539;
  540; 547; 550; 552; 560; 563; 570; 574; 583; 604; 617; 644; 658; 673;
  690; 712; 735; 740; 790; 821; 826; 852; 860; 874; 888; 890; 894; 897;
  904; 909; 919; 925; 926; 944; 946; 951; 961; 973; 1001; 1010; 1030
  W 3; 6; 13; 52; 65; 67; 69; 70; 91; 99; 104; 107; 120; 124; 125; 179; 210;
  277; 307; 314; 379; 425; 468; 522; 543; 626; 705; 732; 845; 849